PHYSICS

FOR KIDS

49 Easy Experiments with Optics

PHYSICS
FOR KIDS

49 Easy Experiments with Optics

Robert W. Wood

Illustrations by Steve Hoeft

TAB Books
Division of McGraw-Hill, Inc.
New York   San Francisco   Washington, D.C.   Auckland   Bogotá
Caracas   Lisbon   London   Madrid   Mexico City   Milan
Montreal   New Delhi   San Juan   Singapore
Sydney   Tokyo   Toronto

pbk 4 5 6 7 8 9 10 11 12 DOC/DOC 9 9 8 7 6 5
hc   1 2 3 4 5 6   7   8   9 DOC/DOC 9 9 8 7 6 5 4 3 2 1 0

Library of Congress Cataloging-in-Publication Data

Wood, Robert W., 1933-
    Physics for kids : 49 easy experiments with optics / by Robert W.
Wood.
        p.   cm.
    Summary: Provides instructions for forty-nine experiments in
optics, including ''How to Bend Light Waves with Your Fingers,'' ''How
to Make a Prism,'' and ''How to Build a Refracting Telescope.''
    ISBN 0-8306-8402-6   ISBN 0-8306-3402-9 (pbk.)
    1. Optics—Experiments—Juvenile literature. [1. Optics-
-Experiments.   2. Experiments.] I. Title.
QC381.W88 1990
535′.078—dc20   89-49447
                                                   CIP
                                                   AC

Acquisitions Editor: Kimberly Tabor
Book Editor: Lori Flaherty
Director of Production: Katherine G. Brown
Cover Photograph by Susan Riley, Harrisonburg, Virginia

Contents

Introduction

Physics is the science that deals with the natural world around us. It tells us how and why a mirror works, why we can't see in the dark, and how birds are able to fly. Physics is such a broad and fascinating science that it is divided into several fields to better understand it—mechanics, heat, optics, electricity and magnetism, and sound. These studies sometimes overlap, however. For instance, someone studying mechanics might need to understand heat because of the friction of moving parts, or a student of electricity might need to study optics to better understand photo cells. Students studying electricity and magnetism to learn why a telephone worked would also have to learn how sound waves vibrate objects that send electrical signals.

This book opens the door to one of the most exciting worlds of physics—the science of optics. Optics is the study of light: What it is, how it behaves, and how we can put it to work for us. Most of us take light for granted, but it is an amazing phenomenon that was once a great mystery. Sunlight governs our daily lives—how we will dress, where we will go, and how we will spend our time. It is also the only source of energy for plants. Without sunlight, there would be no life on Earth. Coal that is now burned for fuel is the remains of plants that were given energy from the sun thousands of years ago. It is no wonder, then, why the study of optics is so important.

Many years ago, light was thought to be something that travelled from our eyes to the object we saw. Then light was studied scientifically, and the science of optics was developed. Telescopes and microscopes were developed during the 1500s and 1600s.

In 1666, Isaac Newton, an English mathematician and physicist, sent a beam of white light through a glass prism. The beam separated into various colors resembling a rainbow. This band of colored lights is called a spectrum. Newton showed that white light was really made up of lights of different colors. Further experimenting led Newton to conclude that light was made up of tiny particles he called corpuscles, and that light travelled in a straight line (although we know that light does not exactly travel in a straight line). About the same time, a Dutch physicist, Christian Huygens, argued that light travelled in waves.

In 1860, English physicist James Clerk Maxwell developed the theory that light was electromagnetic. He believed that light travelled in waves and that it was electrical in nature instead of mechanical like sound waves.

In 1900, Max Planck, a German physicist, established the idea that light is made up of little packages of energy called quanta. This led to the development of the quantum theory, which states that light travels in waves but is corpuscular in nature. So apparently, Newton and Huygens were both right.

The speed of light has been measured at slightly more than 186,000 miles per second. This means that if the sun suddenly went out, it would be about eight minutes before we knew it. What's even more amazing, if you could sit on the North Star and look at the Earth through a powerful telescope, you might see the first of a few scattered settlements along the Atlantic Coast or you could watch the beginning of the European migration to the New World in about 1529. Because of the vast distances in space, a unit called light-year was adopted. This is the distance light travels in one year, or about six billion miles.

Our most important light source is the sun. Early civilizations used flaming torches, then later developed oil lamps and candles. Gas lights were developed next, then mantles were invented. The material of the mantle gave off a brilliant glow when it was heated by the gas flames. The incandescent lamp (regular light bulb) we use today uses a metal filament that is heated to the glowing point by electricity.

Today, many forms of energy are turned into light. These advances in harnessing the power of light allows hospitals, factories, and transportation systems to operate around the clock. The science of optics is also responsible for dramatic advances in electronics and has allowed us to build more powerful microscopes and telescopes, which help us to better understand the universe around us and the tiny protons and electrons of simple matter. The experiments in this book are an easy introduction into the study of optics. You'll learn what light is, where it comes from, and some of the ways you can use it.

Be sure to read the *Symbols Used in This Book* section that follows before you begin any experiment. It warns you of all the safety precautions you should consider before you begin a project and whether or not you should have a teacher or parent help you. Keep safety in mind, and you are sure to have a rewarding first experience in the fascinating world of physics.

Although it is not necessary, I would advise you to do the experiments in order. Some of the principles of optics you learn in the first few experiments will provide you with some of the basic understanding of light and help you to do later experiments.

Symbols Used in This Book

Carefully look over the symbols key below before beginning any experiment. These symbols mean that you should use extra safety precautions, or that some experiments require adult supervision. Before proceeding, *always* refer to this key whenever you see a warning symbol.

Science experiments can be fun and exciting, but safety should always be a first consideration. Parents and teachers are encouraged to participate with their children and students. Adult supervision is advised for very young children. Use common sense and make safety the first consideration, and you will have a safe, fun, educational, and rewarding experience.

 Materials or tools used in this experiment could be dangerous in young hands. Adult supervision is recommended. Children should be instructed on the care and handling of sharp tools or combustible or toxic materials and how to protect surfaces.

 Exercise caution around any open flame or very hot surface such as a stove or hot plate. Adult supervision recommended. Children should be instructed on how to handle hot materials and protect clothing, hair, and surfaces.

 Electricity is used in this experiment. Young children should be supervised and older children cautioned about the hazards of electricity.

 Protective safety goggles should be worn to protect against shattering glass or other hazards that could damage the eyes.

EXPERIMENTS WITH OPTICS

Experiment 1

Materials

- ☐ candle mounted in a dish or metal lid and matches
- ☐ 3 pieces of thin cardboard or poster board (about 4 × 5 inches)
- ☐ 3 supports for cardboard
- ☐ small nail

Determining that Light Travels in a Straight Line

Stack and align the three 4 × 5 cards together and punch a small hole in the center of all three cards with the nail as shown in Fig. 1-1.

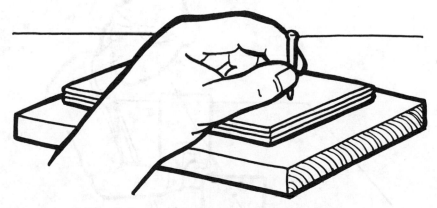

Fig. 1-1. *Punch a hole through the three cards.*

Place the candle on a table and stand one card upright about 12 inches from the candle with the support (blocks, books, etc.) as shown in Fig. 1-2. Carefully light the candle and sight through the hole in the card to the flame of the candle. Be careful handling the candle because hot wax can burn. Tie up loose hair or clothing that could come in contact with the flame. Stand the second card upright about 12 inches from the first and sight through the holes in both cards to the flame (Fig. 1-3). Stand the third card in the same manner and sight through all three holes to the candle flame. All holes must be lined up in a straight line (see Fig. 1-4). Once all of the holes are aligned, you will be able to see the light

Fig. 1-2. *Sight through the hole of the first card.*

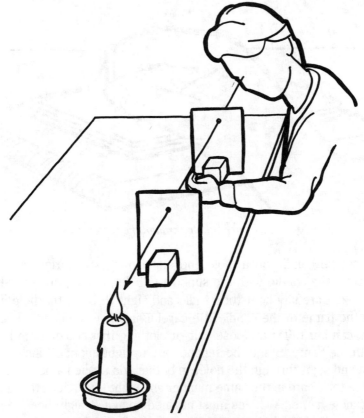

Fig. 1-3. *Align the holes of both cards.*

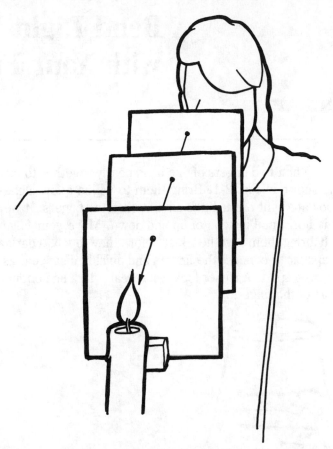

Fig. 1-4. *Light must travel in a straight line to reach your eye.*

from the candle. But if any one of the cards are moved slightly, you won't be able to see the flame through the holes. This means that the light travels in a straight line so all holes must be in line if the light is to get through.

Remember to blow the candle out when you're done. It's a good idea not to move the candle until the wax cools because hot wax can burn.

Experiment 2

Materials

- ☐ light source
- ☐ two fingers

How to Bend Light Waves with Your Fingers

Place the first two fingers of one hand nearly together to form a narrow slit as shown in Fig. 2-1. Bring them to within a few inches of one eye and look at a light through the slit between the fingers. It works best if the slit is horizontal instead of up and down. Move your fingers apart then slowly bring them together. Just before they touch, a dark area will suddenly appear to connect the fingers and quickly disappear as the fingers are moved apart. A closer look will reveal a dark line outlining some of the areas of the fingers.

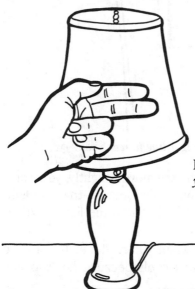

Fig. 2-1. *Barely separate your fingers and you can see bent light waves.*

As the light waves enter the opening of the slit, some of the waves striking the edge of the fingers bend slightly and break up into the dark area behind the fingers. This is called diffraction. When one pattern of waves overlap and combine with another, they produce either a stronger or weaker wave. This is called interference. The dark area that suddenly appeared is where these waves came together.

Experiment 3

Materials

☐ mirror
☐ flashlight

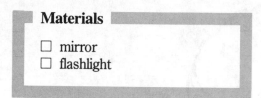

How the Eye's Pupil Adjusts for Light Conditions

Look into a mirror in a normally lighted room and notice the size of the dark circle in the center of your eye (Fig. 3-1). This is the pupil. Briefly shine the flashlight into one eye as shown in Fig. 3-2. Look into the mirror again, and the dark circle quickly becomes smaller (Fig. 3-3). After the light is turned off, the pupil grows larger and returns to its original size.

The pupil is light sensitive. It operates much like the shutters on a window or the shutter on a camera. It automatically adjusts to allow the right amount of light into the eye.

Fig. 3-1. *Look at the size of the pupil in your eye.*

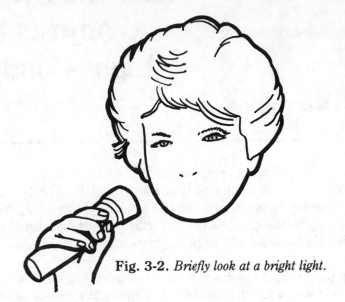

Fig. 3-2. *Briefly look at a bright light.*

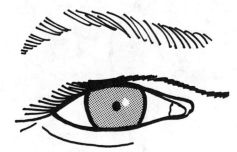

Fig. 3-3. *The pupil became smaller to let in less light.*

Experiment 4

How to Make Pinhole Glasses

Materials

- [ ] cardboard from a cereal box
- [ ] eye glasses
- [ ] scissors
- [ ] pencil

Completely unfold an empty cereal box and trace the outline of the glasses on the dull inside part (Fig. 4-1). Cut out the glasses and trim them to fit snugly. Make a pinhole in the center of each cardboard lens with the tip of a pencil as shown in Fig. 4-2. Now try them out on a printed page. If you normally wear glasses for nearsightedness or farsightedness, you should notice a remarkable difference (Fig. 4-3).

The pinhole glasses work on the same principle as the pinhole camera. The pinhole camera has an infinite field of depth. This means that it can produce a sharper image up close or at a distance. The pinhole glasses convert the eye into a pinhole camera. Normally, the eye automatically produces the same effect, but for eyes suffering from nearsightedness or farsightedness, the pinholes allow the light rays to converge to a point of focus.

Fig. 4-1. *Cut out the glasses from thin cardboard.*

9

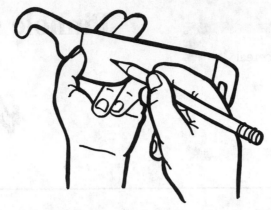

Fig. 4-2. *Punch a small hole in the center of each lens.*

Fig. 4-3. *Eyes that are nearsighted or farsighted will have improved vision.*

Experiment 5

Materials

☐ 2 lenses from discarded Polaroid sunglasses
☐ lamp

How Polaroid Sunglasses Reduce Glare

Place one lens over the other and look through both toward the lamp as shown in Fig. 5-1. You will see that much of the light gets through both lenses. Now hold one lens and slowly rotate the other. When it becomes exactly upright, practically no light gets through (Fig. 5-2).

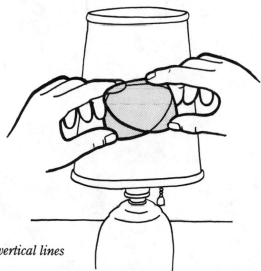

Fig. 5-1. *Polarized lenses have vertical lines that reduce glare.*

The lenses of Polaroid sunglasses are made up of vertical lines. In this experiment, the lens in front polarizes the light coming through it. If the lines in the second lens are lined up with the lines in the front lens, the polarized light is able to pass through. But when the second lens was rotated, the first lens still produced a polarized beam but was unable to pass through the second lens and most of the light was shut out.

Light travelling in waves that strike a shiny surface is reflected off, producing a glare around the object. The lines in the lenses form a grating that acts like a filter to reduce the glare.

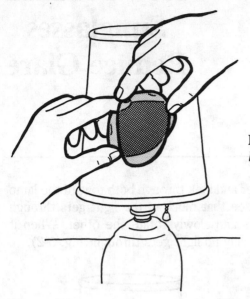

Fig. 5-2. *If the lenses are crossed, little light gets through.*

Experiment 6

How to Make a Solar Eclipse

Slide the disk (the moon) about half way into the paper clip (Fig. 6-1), then insert the end of the paper clip into the end of the straw as shown in Fig. 6-2. Stand the straw upright using the spool for a base, and place it on a table (Fig. 6-3). Next, cover the lens of the flashlight (the sun) with a piece of wax paper and hold secure with a rubber band (Fig. 6-4). Using books for a support, position the flashlight so it will shine level with the moon as shown in Fig. 6-5. The moon should be about a foot or so from the flashlight. Some adjustments might be necessary. Turn on the flashlight and turn the room lights off. Position yourself so the moon will be about half way between you and the flashlight. Close

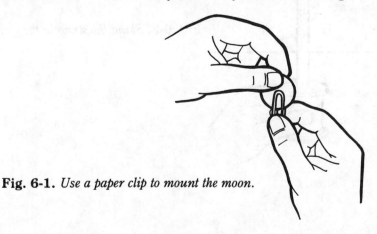

Fig. 6-1. *Use a paper clip to mount the moon.*

one eye, and with the other eye, align the moon so that it almost blocks out the light (Fig. 6-6). The moon covers the sun, but the corona can still be seen. This is a fiery ring that is seen outlining the moon during a total eclipse.

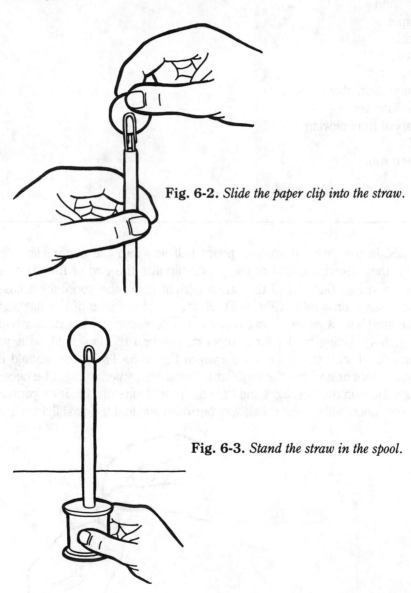

Fig. 6-2. *Slide the paper clip into the straw.*

Fig. 6-3. *Stand the straw in the spool.*

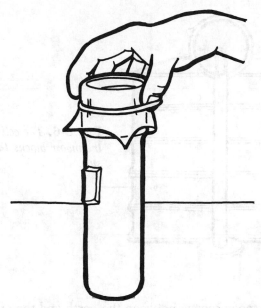

Fig. 6-4. *Cover the lens with wax paper and secure it with a rubber band.*

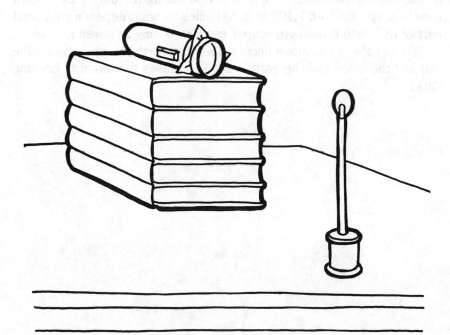

Fig. 6-5. *Use books to position the sun.*

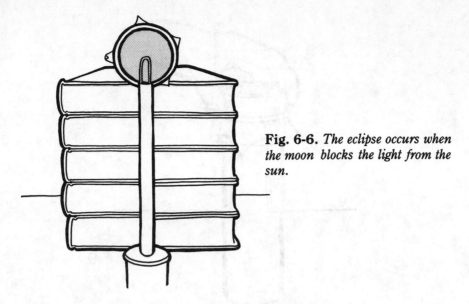

Fig. 6-6. *The eclipse occurs when the moon blocks the light from the sun.*

When the moon moves between the earth and the sun, its shadow makes some areas dark for a brief period during the day. This shadow travels at speeds from 1,100 to 5,000 miles an hour, depending on what part of the earth it falls. An eclipse can last as long as seven minutes.

An eclipse of the moon occurs when the earth moves between the sun and the moon and the earth's shadow causes the moon to become dark.

Experiment 7

Why Stars Twinkle

Using the nail, punch a number of small holes in one side of the cereal box as shown in Fig. 7-1. Turn on the flashlight and place it inside the cereal box as shown in Fig. 7-2. Close the flaps so no light escapes except through the holes. These will be the stars.

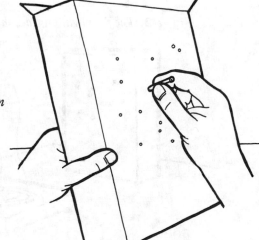

Fig. 7-1. *Punch small holes in one side of the box.*

Place the box at one end of a table or counter. Position the hot plate in the middle of the table and turn out the lights in the room (Fig. 7-3). Be very careful around the hot plate so you don't burn yourself. Be sure to protect the surface beneath it and turn off the hot plate or stove when you are done. Move to the other end of the table and look at the lights from the box through the warm air rising from the hot plate. The tiny lights from the box will twinkle like stars.

Fig. 7-2. *The flashlight provides the light for the stars.*

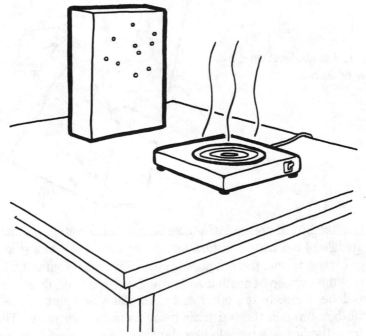

Fig. 7-3. *The warm air causes the stars to twinkle.*

The warm air rising from the stove moves up with varying temperatures. These different temperatures causes the air to have a variety of densities.

When a beam of light travels from the air of one density to another, it bends slightly. When a light beam bends, it is refracted. The earth's atmosphere has varying temperatures and densities. The movement of the layers of the atmosphere bend and scatter starlight so that they seem to twinkle. In space, stars do not twinkle.

Experiment 8

How to Make a Sundial

Materials

- ☐ piece of thin cardboard
- ☐ wood or cardboard base, 12 × 6 inches
- ☐ protractor
- ☐ magnetic compass
- ☐ transparent tape or masking tape

The thin cardboard will be cut into a right-angled triangle called a gnomon, but first you'll need to know the latitude of the place where you live. This is an imaginary line running around the earth, parallel to the equator. They are measured in degrees starting from the equator and going to the poles. The equator has a latitude of 0 degrees, the North Pole has a latitude of 90 degrees north and the South Pole is at 90 degrees south. You can find your latitude on a map of your area. In the United States, this will be somewhere between 30 and 50 degrees.

For example, suppose that your latitude is 40 degrees. This would be the angle for the longest line of the triangle, the sloping part. You would draw the baseline six inches long (see Fig. 8-1). You would then draw the 90 degree corner. This line would be about five inches long. Using the protractor, you would mark off a 40 degree angle from the baseline and draw this line to complete the triangle. This line would be about 7³/₄ inches long. Cut out the triangle. Mark a line across the 12 × 6 inch base dividing it into two, six-inch halves. Draw a semicircle with a six-inch radius (Fig. 8-2). Using tape, mount the triangle on the wood base. The base of the triangle should be on the line across the middle of the wood base. The sloping 40 degree side of the triangle should be pointing to the center of the semicircle.

Place the sundial outside and using the magnetic compass align the triangle north and south (Fig. 8-3). Position the sundial so that the 40 degree angle aims skyward toward the north. This means that the back side, or tallest part of the triangle will be pointing north. To be more accurate the sundial should be aligned true north instead of magnetic north. Often streets run true north, south, east, or west. Or you could align it with the North star at night.

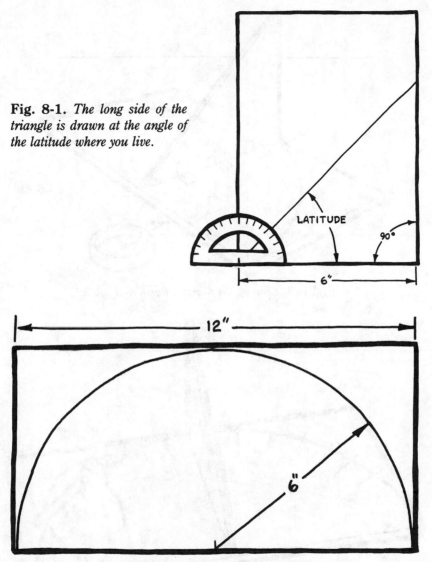

Fig. 8-1. *The long side of the triangle is drawn at the angle of the latitude where you live.*

Fig. 8-2. *Mark the base off in a half circle.*

After the sundial has been properly positioned, every hour mark the location of the shadow on the base (Fig. 8-4). You should have numbers starting about six at the beginning of the semicircle going up to 12 noon at the back of the triangle, then going on to about six in the afternoon, at the end of the semicircle. The 12 or so marks should be an equal distance around the half circle. Your sundial will now tell you the time on sunny days.

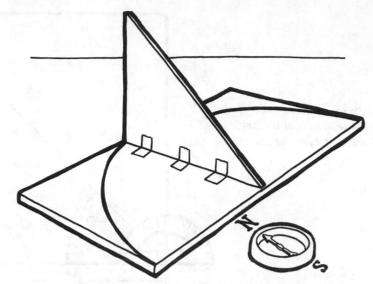

Fig. 8-3. *Line up the sundial north and south.*

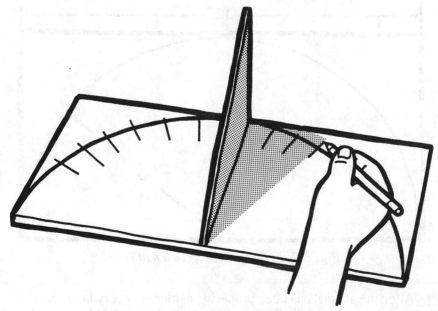

Fig. 8-4. *Mark off the sundial in hours.*

Experiment 9

Materials

- ☐ sunny day
- ☐ flagpole
- ☐ tape measure
- ☐ yardstick
- ☐ pencil and paper or calculator

How a Shadow Can Be Used to Measure an Object's Height

Using the tape measure, measure the length of the shadow of the flagpole and convert this number into inches (Fig. 9-1). Stand the yardstick upright on the ground so that it casts a shadow like the flagpole as

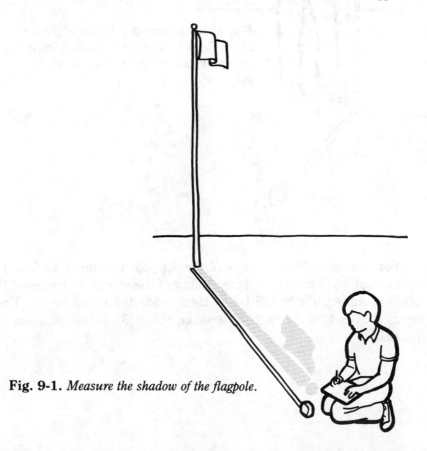

Fig. 9-1. *Measure the shadow of the flagpole.*

shown in Fig. 9-2. Measure the length of the shadow cast by the yardstick. Now multiply the length of the flagpole's shadow by 36 inches (the height of the yardstick) and divide that number by the length of the shadow of the yardstick. The results will be the approximate height of the flagpole.

Fig. 9-2. *Measure the shadow of the yardstick. Flagpoles shadow × height of stick ÷ shadow of stick = approximate height of flagpole.*

For example, if the shadow of the flagpole measured 14 feet 11 inches, that's 179 inches, and the shadow of the yardstick measured 19 inches, simply multiply 179 by 36 then divide the result by 19. This means the height of the flagpole would be about 339 inches, or about 28 feet tall.

Experiment 10

How to Make a Solar Still

Materials

- ☐ small shovel
- ☐ bowl
- ☐ clear, plastic sheet
- ☐ marbles or small stones
- ☐ sunny day

Dig a hole in the ground about 12 inches deep and about 18 inches across as shown in Fig. 10-1. Place the bowl in the center of the bottom of the hole. Spread the clear plastic sheet over the hole with a marble or stone in the center (see Fig. 10-2). Allow the plastic to sag into the hole a couple of inches above the bowl. Place the remaining marbles or stones around the outer edge of the plastic to hold it in place. Cover these weights with the dirt from the hole to help trap air in the hole as shown in Fig. 10-3. After a period of time, depending on moisture in the ground and the heat of the sun, water will begin to drip into the bowl.

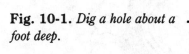

Fig. 10-1. *Dig a hole about a foot deep.*

Sunlight shines through the plastic and warms the earth inside the hole. This causes the moisture in the ground to evaporate. The water vapor then condenses and forms droplets on the underside of the plastic. The drops then run down to the lowest point and drip into the bowl.

Fig. 10-2. *Spread plastic over the hole.*

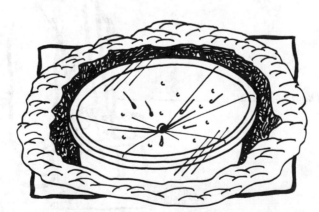

Fig. 10-3. *Heat causes moisture to condense on the bottom side of the plastic.*

Experiment 11

Light Diffraction

Materials

- ☐ dark colored marble
- ☐ thread
- ☐ glue
- ☐ flashlight
- ☐ box support for flashlight
- ☐ piece of white paper
- ☐ transparent tape

Attach one end of the thread to the marble with the glue as shown in Fig. 11-1. While the glue is drying, place the flashlight on the box under the edge of a table or an open countertop (Fig. 11-2). Suspend the marble from the edge of the table so that it is about three inches in front of, and exactly in line with, the beam from the flashlight (see Fig. 11-3).

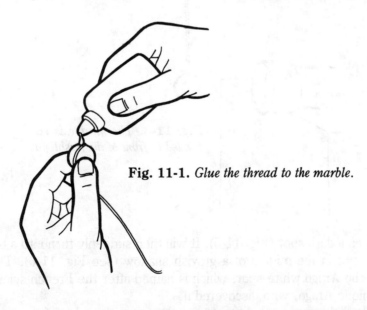

Fig. 11-1. *Glue the thread to the marble.*

Secure the thread to the table with a small strip of tape. When the suspended marble is still, place the white paper directly behind the marble to form a dark, sharp shadow as shown in Fig. 11-4. Now, slowly move the paper away, gradually reducing the size of the shadow until it

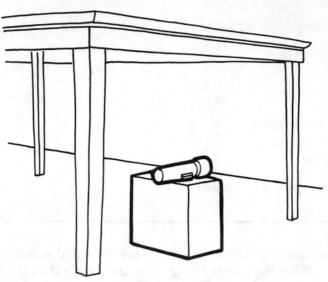

Fig. 11-2. *A box can be used to support the flashlight.*

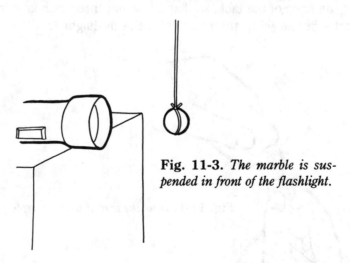

Fig. 11-3. *The marble is suspended in front of the flashlight.*

becomes a dark spot (Fig. 11-5). It will then suddenly turn into a bright white spot in the middle of a grayish shadow (see Fig. 11-6). This is called the Arago white spot, which is named after the French scientist, Dominique Arago, who discovered it.

The light waves are diffracted as they pass the edge of the marble. The light bends around the marble to form a white spot in its shadow.

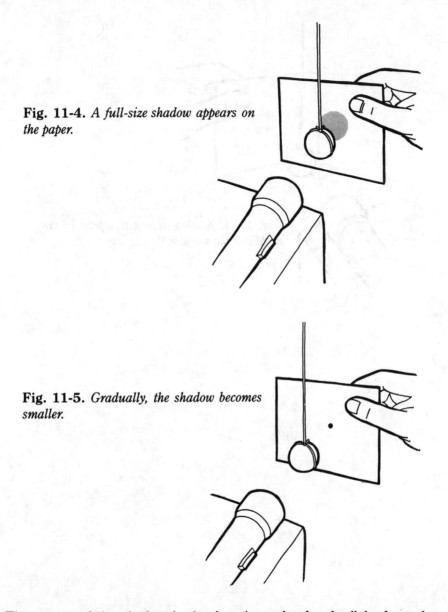

Fig. 11-4. *A full-size shadow appears on the paper.*

Fig. 11-5. *Gradually, the shadow becomes smaller.*

The center of the shadow is the focusing point for the light from the edge of the marble. The rest of the area of the shadow is darker because the light waves arriving there are diffracted differently and are travelling different distances. They interfere with each other and are not in focus.

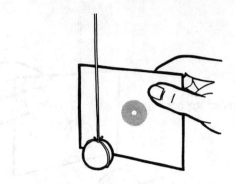

Fig. 11-6. *A white spot will appear in the middle of the shadow.*

Experiment 12   The Floating Finger

Hold together the ends of a finger from each hand about arms length in front of you (Fig. 12-1). Look under your fingers at some distant object. The fingers will now appear in three sections (Fig. 12-2). Separate the fingers slightly and a finger with two fingernails will seem to be suspended between your two fingers (Fig. 12-3).

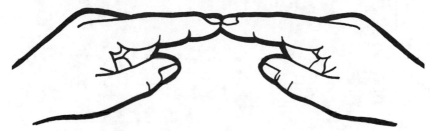

Fig. 12-1. *Touch two fingers together and focus on a distant object.*

Fig. 12-2. *You should see what appears to be a third finger with two nails.*

Fig. 12-3. *Separate your fingers a little and a third finger will seem to be suspended between your fingers.*

This is an optical illusion caused by the path of light travelling from the distant object to the two eyes.

When light rays strike the curved surface of the cornea, they are partially bent, or refracted, toward each other through the pupil and lens to a point called the focus. If the focus is on the retina, you see a clear image. Light rays coming from an object close to the eye are divergent, or spread out. Light rays coming from a distant object are almost parallel. The lens cannot focus divergent light rays from an object close by and parallel rays from a distant object on the retina at the same time.

Experiment 13

Looking through a Hole in Your Hand

Materials

☐ cardboard tube from paper towel or rolled sheet of paper

Place the tube in front of one eye like a telescope and look at a distant object (Fig. 13-1). Now bring the palm of your free hand up next to the tube (Fig. 13-2). A hole will appear allowing you to see the distant object through your hand (Fig. 13-3).

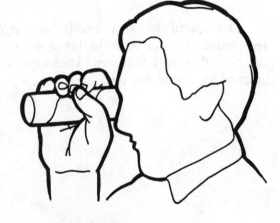

Fig. 13-1. *Sight through the tube at a distant object.*

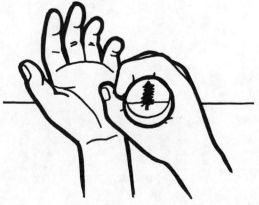

Fig. 13-2. *Place your hand next to the tube.*

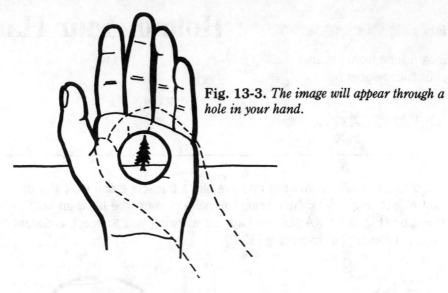

Fig. 13-3. *The image will appear through a hole in your hand.*

This optical illusion is seen because our eyes see two images that are combined by our brain. In this case, one eye sees the distant object and the other sees the hand. These two images are combined by the brain to create the illusion.

Experiment 14

Candle Burning under Water

Materials

- [ ] cardboard box (about $1^1/_2$ × 2 feet wide and about $1^1/_2$ feet high)
- [ ] piece of cardboard (about $1^1/_2$ × $2^1/_2$ feet)
- [ ] dull, black paint
- [ ] glass from picture frame (about 8 × 10 inch)
- [ ] transparent tape
- [ ] paint brush
- [ ] old newspapers
- [ ] 2 identical drinking glasses or glass jars
- [ ] small candle and matches
- [ ] water
- [ ] utility knife

Carefully cut the flaps from the top of the box and fit the long piece of cardboard inside, upright from the left front corner to the right rear corner. This will divide the box equally into two diagonal shaped compartments (see Fig. 14-1). Very carefully cut a small viewing window (about 6 inches square) in the front left-half of the box as shown in Fig. 14-2 (the side where the dividing cardboard meets the corner). Do not hold the cardboard against you while you cut, you could easily cut yourself. Also, be sure you cut on a surface that won't scratch or mar.

Sight through the window down the left half of the box. You will only be able to see the cardboard divider. Remove the divider and cut a window about 7 × 9 inches that will allow you to see straight through to the left, rear-side of the box (Fig. 14-3). Paint the divider and the inside of the box dull black. Be sure to spread old newspapers under the box to protect the tabletop or counter. After the paint has dried, tape the 8-by-10-inch glass to the opening in the divider. Place the divider back in the box (Fig. 14-4).

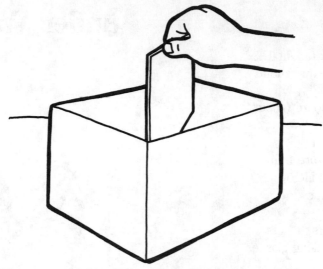

Fig. 14-1. *Divide the box diagonally into two compartments.*

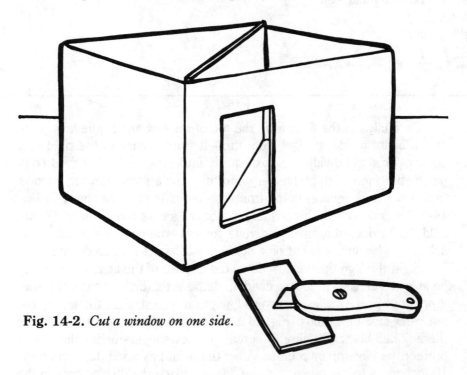

Fig. 14-2. *Cut a window on one side.*

Fig. 14-3. *Cut an opening for the glass in the divider and paint the inside dull black.*

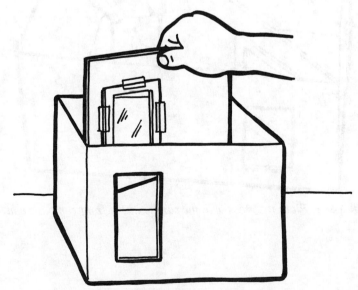

Fig. 14-4. *Place the divider back in the box.*

Mount the candle in the bottom of one of glasses and light it, or have an adult light it. Hot wax can burn. Also, tie up any loose hair or clothing that could ignite near flame. Place the glass and the candle in the center of the first compartment (Fig. 14-5). Place the empty glass in the center of the rear compartment (Fig. 14-6). Sight through the viewing window through the glass and you should see both glasses. Align them so that the two appear as one (Fig. 14-7). Now, while someone looks through the viewing window, slowly pour water into the empty glass in the rear compartment as shown in Fig. 14-8. They will see what appears to be a candle burning in a glass of water. Be sure to extinguish the flame and let it cool before you try to move it.

This optical illusion is caused by light reflecting from one side of the glass window. This creates the image of the glass with the candle while you are still able to see through the window to the glass with the water.

Fig. 14-5. *Place the glass with the candle in the front compartment.*

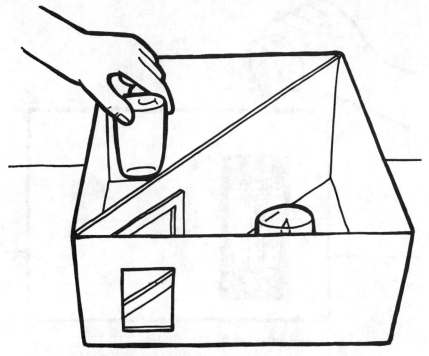

Fig. 14-6. *Place the empty glass in the rear compartment.*

Fig. 14-7. *Line up both glasses so they appear as one.*

Fig. 14-8. *Pour water in the rear glass.*

Experiment 15   Persistence of Vision

In a dark room, turn on the lamp and stare at the bulb for about ten seconds. You should be several feet from the lamp (Fig. 15-1). Switch off the lamp and you will continue to see the lighted bulb.

Fig. 15-1. *Look at a light in a dark room, then turn the light off.*

Your eyes continue to see an object for a very brief period of time after the object is no longer visible. This persistence of vision allows us to see the motion in pictures taken by movie and television cameras. Scenes captured on film are made up of a series of still pictures while those displayed on a television consist of lines scanned by an electron beam across the phosphorus screen of a television picture tube.

Experiment 16

Putting a Bird in a Cage

Cut a small disk (about 1½ inches) from the cardboard. Use the nail to make two holes close together on each side as shown in Fig. 16-1. Thread one of the strings through the holes on one side and tie the ends together (see Fig. 16-2). This will make a loop for one side of the disk. Repeat the steps and make a loop for the other side.

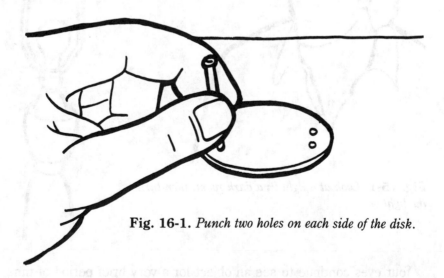

Fig. 16-1. *Punch two holes on each side of the disk.*

Draw a bird cage in the center of the disk (Fig. 16-3). On the other side, draw a bird (Fig. 16-4). Loop the strings over a finger or two on each hand and whirl the disk around to start it spinning. This bird will appear inside the cage as shown in Fig. 16-5. This is because the persistence of vision will continue to see the bird while the cage is in view.

42

Fig. 16-2. *Make loops for each side of the disk.*

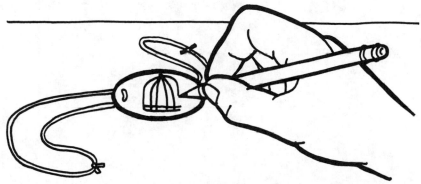

Fig. 16-3. *Draw a bird cage on the disk.*

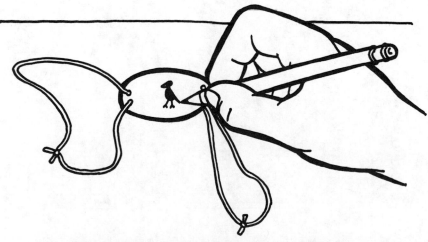

Fig. 16-4. *Draw a bird on the other side of the disk.*

Putting a Bird in a Cage

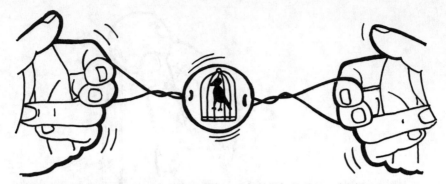

Fig. 16-5. *The spinning disk will make the bird appear inside the cage.*

Experiment 17

Why Light is White

Materials

- ☐ 3 flashlights that produce a small beam
- ☐ 3 pieces each of red, blue, and green cellophane
- ☐ 3 rubber bands
- ☐ dark room
- ☐ sheet of white paper

Cover the lens of one of the flashlights with three layers of red cellophane and fasten it in place with a rubber band (see Fig. 17-1). Cover another flashlight with three layers of blue cellophane and the third with green.

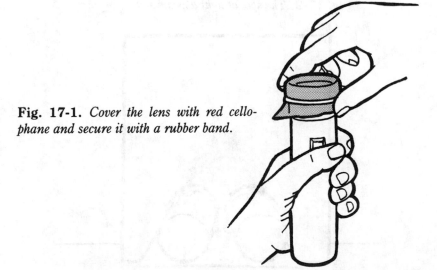

Fig. 17-1. *Cover the lens with red cellophane and secure it with a rubber band.*

In a dark room shine the red light on the white paper. This will make a red spot of light. Place the flashlight on a book or some other support so that the spot will remain steady on the paper as shown in Fig. 17-2. Now, position the green light in a similar manner so it makes a green spot on top of the red one (see Fig. 17-3). The red and green spots

Fig. 17-2. *The spot of light appears red.*

Fig. 17-3. *A red spot and a green spot produce a yellow spot.*

Fig. 17-4. *Red, green, and blue cellophane produce a white spot.*

together will produce a yellow spot. Next, shine the blue light on the yellow spot and the spot becomes almost white (Fig. 17-4).

It is almost impossible to produce a true white spot using ordinary equipment, because the colors coming through the cellophane are not true spectrum colors. A spectrum is a rainbow band of colors when a beam of white light passes through a glass prism. All of the colors found in the spectrum, when mixed together, produce white light.

Experiment 18

How to Make a Color Disk

Materials

- [ ] small piece of poster board
- [ ] scissors
- [ ] watercolor paints
- [ ] small brush
- [ ] old newspapers
- [ ] string (about 3 to 4 feet long)
- [ ] compass
- [ ] ruler

Set the compass for a two-inch radius and draw a four-inch circle on the poster board (Fig. 18-1). Keeping the compass set at two inches, make six marks, equal distances around the outer edge of the circle.

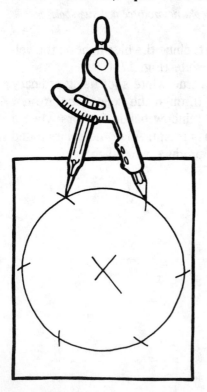

Fig. 18-1. *Use the compass to measure around the circle.*

With the ruler, draw lines across the circle, through the center, from one mark to another (Fig. 18-2). This will divide the circle into six equal parts. Cut out the circle and make two small holes about a half inch apart near the center (Fig. 18-3). These holes will be used for the loop of string.

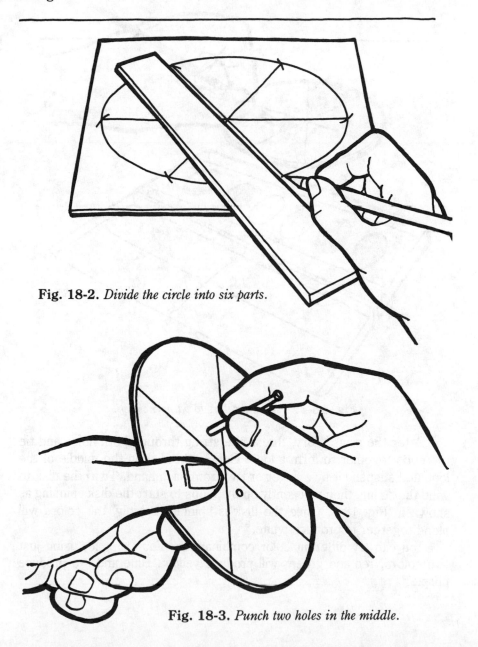

Fig. 18-2. *Divide the circle into six parts.*

Fig. 18-3. *Punch two holes in the middle.*

Spread old newspapers on a table or countertop, and using the watercolors, paint one pie-shaped part blue. Now going clockwise around, paint the next part green, the next yellow, then orange, red, and violet (Fig. 18-4).

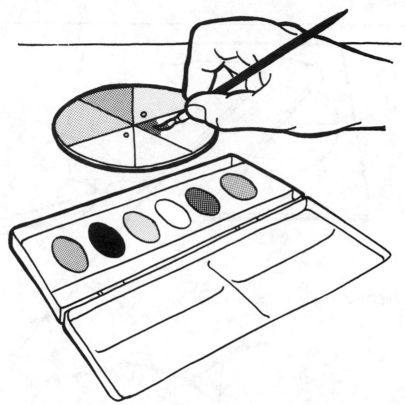

Fig. 18-4. *Use watercolors to paint the disk.*

After the paint is dry, thread the string through both holes and tie the ends together to form a loop. Center the disk in the middle of the loop and suspend it by a finger or two from each hand. Twirl the disk to wind the string, then pull gently on the loops to start the disk spinning as shown in Fig. 18-5. Once the disk is spinning rapidly, the colors will blend together to produce white.

You can try different color combinations. For example, using just two colors, red and green, will produce yellow. Blue and red produce purple.

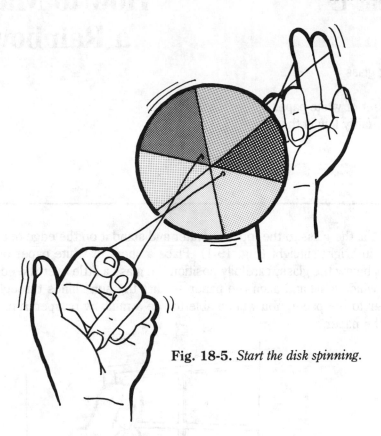

Fig. 18-5. *Start the disk spinning.*

Experiment 19

How to Make a Rainbow

Materials

- ☐ drinking glass
- ☐ water
- ☐ large sheet of white paper
- ☐ sunlight, fairly low in the sky

Fill the glass to the top with water and stand it on the edge of a window in bright sunlight (Fig. 19-1). Place a sheet of white paper on the floor below the glass, carefully position the glass a little over the edge of the window sill and align the paper so that the sun shines through the water to the paper. You will be able to see a rainbow or spectrum band on the paper.

Fig. 19-1. *Fill a glass with water and place it in sunlight to produce a rainbow.*

52

Rainbows are formed when raindrops refract sunlight. This breaks the white sunlight into seven colors and reflects it back. The seven colors are red, orange, yellow, green, blue, indigo, and violet.

Experiment 20

How to Make a Prism

Materials

- ☐ square bowl or pan
- ☐ water
- ☐ small mirror
- ☐ bright sunlight
- ☐ white paper

Fill the bowl with about one inch of water and place it on a table in bright sunlight. Stand the mirror inside the bowl against the side of the bowl facing the sun. Some adjusting might be necessary, but the mirror should be slanted about 45 degrees as shown in Fig. 20-1. Hold the sheet of white paper so that the sun's rays are reflected on it. You might have to adjust this also. You will be able to see a rainbow of colors. Stir the water a little with your finger, and the rainbow will disappear.

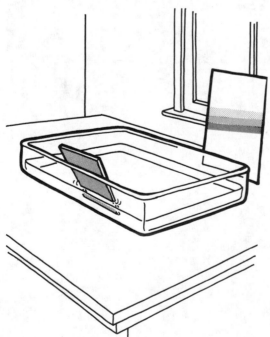

Fig. 20-1. *A mirror in water will separate colors.*

Light travels at a slower speed through water and glass than it does in air. When the light slows down, it also changes directions slightly. The beam of white light is reflected at an angle through a "wedge" of water between the mirror and the surface of the water. The wedge acts like a prism. The colors are bent at different angles and travel at different speeds. Red light bends the least and violet light bends greatest. The beam spreads and the colors separate according to their individual wave lengths. When the water is disturbed, the side of the prism is so distorted that the different wave lengths mix back together into white light.

Experiment 21

How Filters Change the Color of Light

Set the prism up in sunlight so that it casts the rainbow pattern on the white paper. Place the piece of red cellophane between the prism and the white paper as shown in Fig. 21-1. The cellophane will act like a light filter. Notice the color on the white paper. Now try the green and then the blue cellophane filters. In each case, the color on the white paper was the same color of the filter. The red filter would only allow red light through. The green would pass only green light and the same with blue. The filters absorbed all of the other colors.

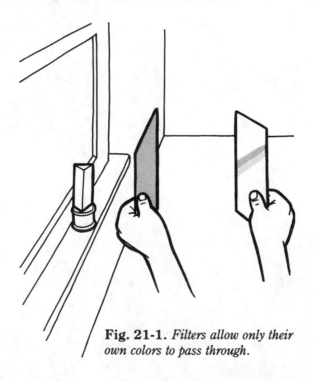

Fig. 21-1. *Filters allow only their own colors to pass through.*

Experiment 22

☐ pencil
☐ drinking glass
☐ water

The Broken Pencil in Water

Fill the glass nearly to the top with water. Place the pencil in the water so that it slants across the inside of the glass as shown in Fig. 22-1. Notice the part of the pencil where it enters the water. It appears broken and slightly larger. This is because the light that shines on the upper part of the pencil first strikes the pencil then travels to your eyes through air and the top part of the glass. This light is only reflected and not bent. But the light that allows you to see the part of the pencil below the water must travel through the water, the glass, and then the air to reach your eyes. The light rays are bent. This slows the light rays just enough so that they reach your eyes slightly after the ones from the part of the pencil above the water. This time difference is enough to distort the image. The distortion is called refraction.

The pencil below the water also appears larger. This is because the water and curvature of the glass magnify the image.

Fig. 22-1. *Bent light rays cause the pencil to appear broken.*

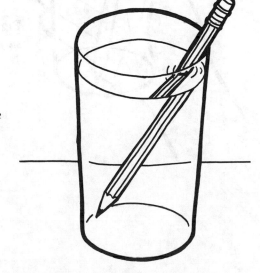

Experiment 23

The Disappearing Pencil

Fill the glass about three-fourths full of water. Place the pencil in the glass and hold it at arm's length in front of you, slightly above your head. Look up at the pencil and the area below the surface of the water. The pencil and nothing else can be seen above the water (see Fig. 23-1). If you look at the surface at an angle from below, the surface acts like a mirror. The light rays are reflected back. If you hold the glass straight overhead, the mirror effect goes away. The light rays are not reflected back.

Fig. 23-1. *The bottom side of the surface acts like a mirror.*

Experiment 24

The Moving Coin

Place the coin in the bowl at the edge where the bowl starts to slope upward as shown in Fig. 24-1. This will be a reference point. Look at the coin from an angle above the lip of the bowl. Position your head so that you can only see the outer edge of the coin, keep looking at the coin and very slowly pour water into the bowl (see Figs. 24-2 and 24-3). The coin will appear to move toward the center of the bowl until it is in full view. Check to ensure that the coin hasn't moved by looking at the reference point.

Fig. 24-1. *Place the coin at the edge of the bottom.*

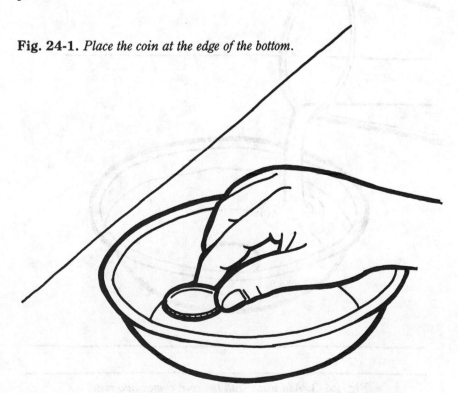

59

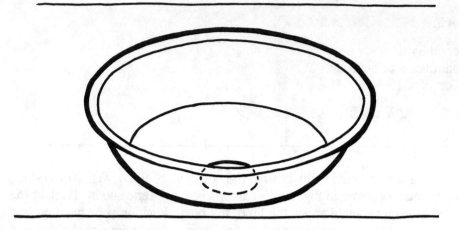

Fig. 24-2. *Sight over the lip of the bowl.*

Fig. 24-3. *Add water and the coin comes into view.*

When there was no water in the bowl, the light travelled in a straight line from the coin to your eyes. As you sighted over the edge of the bowl, only the outer edge of the coin was reflecting light to your eyes. When water was added to the bowl, the light rays were bent, or refracted by the water. The angle of the bending was great enough to allow all of the light reflected from the coin to travel to your eyes.

Experiment 25

Materials

☐ round jar
☐ square canning jar
☐ water
☐ pencil

Comparing Round and Square Glass Containers

Fill both jars about half full of water. Lower the pencil into the square jar first. Place the pencil against the side of the jar closest to you and slowly move it away towards the other side (Fig. 25-1). The pencil will remain about the same size below the water (Fig. 25-2). Now repeat the same steps with the pencil in the round jar. When the pencil is first viewed next to the glass, the part below the surface will be the same size, but as you move it away, it grows steadily larger (Figs. 25-3 and 25-4).

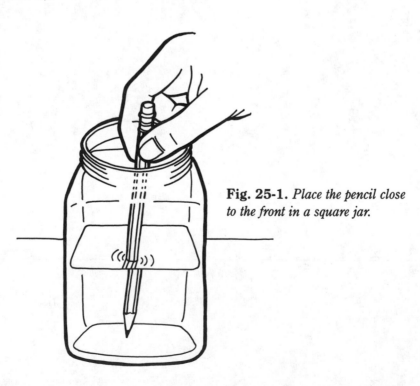

Fig. 25-1. *Place the pencil close to the front in a square jar.*

Fig. 25-2. *Move the pencil to the back of the jar. The pencil doesn't appear much different.*

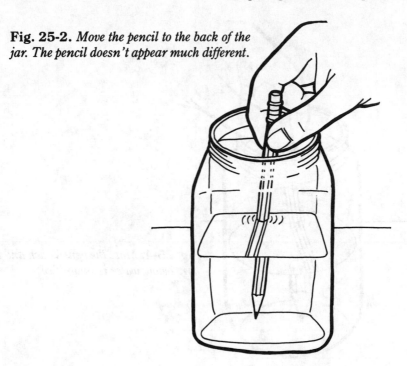

Fig. 25-3. *Place the pencil near the front of a round jar.*

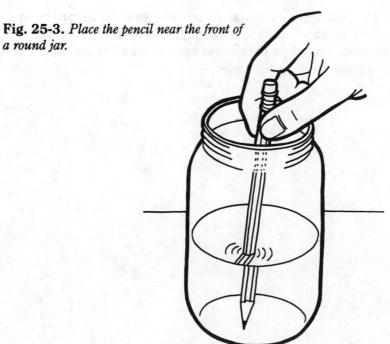

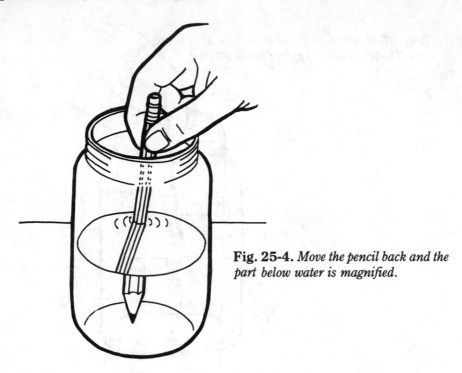

Fig. 25-4. *Move the pencil back and the part below water is magnified.*

The roundness of the jar causes the water to be curved in such a way that the water acts like a magnifying lens. The square jar does not. Food companies often pack items such as cherries and olives in round jars to make them appear larger.

Experiment 26

Materials

- ☐ piece of glass (from picture frame)
- ☐ sheet of white paper
- ☐ drops of water
- ☐ sunlight or flashlight

Dark Spots from Clear Water

Place a few drops of water about a half inch in diameter on the glass as shown in Fig. 26-1. Hold the glass in the sunlight so that the spots cast their shadow on the white paper as shown in Fig. 26-2. Raise and lower the glass to the paper. When the glass is next to the paper, the spots act like magnifying lenses and you see a clear spot below them. As the glass is raised, the bright spot grows smaller and is surrounded by a very dark ring.

The light rays striking the glass pass through evenly, but the rays striking the rounded drops of water are bent. When the rays hit the paper, most of the light can be concentrated in a focal point of bright light, but the remaining light rays are distorted and make up the dark area.

Fig. 26-1. *Drop some water on the glass.*

Fig. 26-2. *Light rays passing through the water are bent.*

Experiment 27

How Light Can Flow Inside Water

Materials

- ☐ empty soda pop can
- ☐ can opener
- ☐ nail
- ☐ flashlight
- ☐ dark room
- ☐ water
- ☐ bucket or pan to catch water

Carefully cut the top from an empty cola can with the can opener and rinse it out with clean water to get rid of the stickiness (Fig. 27-1). With the nail, punch a small hole in the side of the can near the bottom (Fig. 27-2). Fill the can with water and hold your finger over the hole to keep it from leaking (Fig. 27-3). Turn on the flashlight and place the lens against the top of the can as shown in Fig. 27-4.

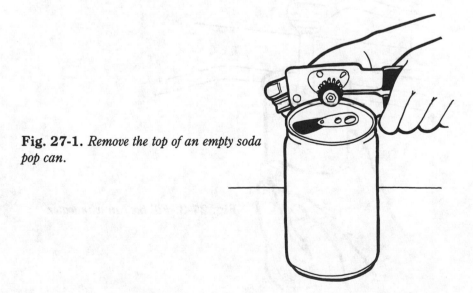

Fig. 27-1. *Remove the top of an empty soda pop can.*

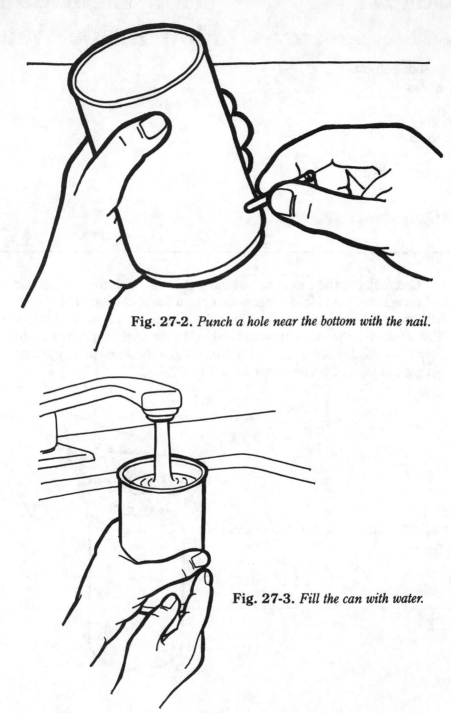

Fig. 27-2. *Punch a hole near the bottom with the nail.*

Fig. 27-3. *Fill the can with water.*

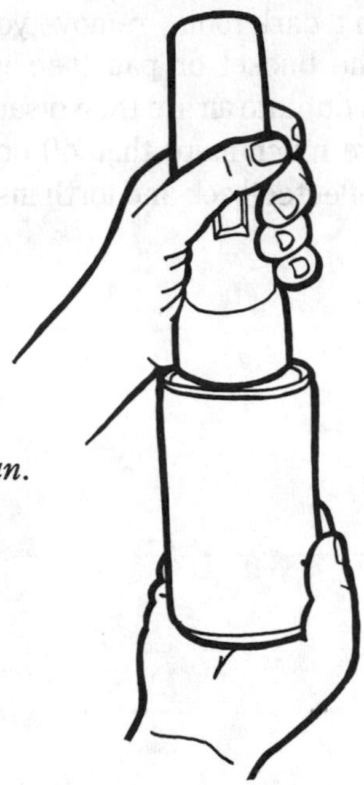

Fig. 27-4. *Shine a light inside the can.*

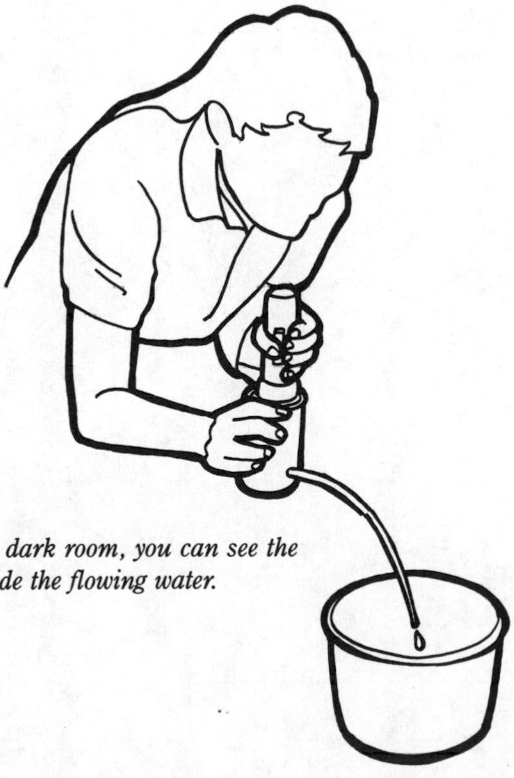

Fig. 27-5. *In a dark room, you can see the light trapped inside the flowing water.*

In a dark room, remove your finger and let the stream of water spill into the bucket or pan (see Fig. 27-5). Notice that the lighted water twists out into an arc then disappears into the pan. The light won't follow a curve much more than 40 or 50 degrees in water. The light is spread and reflected back and forth inside the stream but cannot escape from it.

Experiment 28

How Fiberoptics Work

Materials

☐ piece of plate glass (from picture frame)
☐ flashlight
☐ piece of cardboard (from picture frame)
☐ sheet of white paper

Place the cardboard on a table and lay the glass on top of the cardboard. The dull cardboard is to reduce reflections from under the glass. Slide the end of the sheet of paper about an inch under one end of the glass and curve the paper up to catch the rays of light as shown in Fig. 28-1. Shine the flashlight so that the beam enters the edge of the glass at the other end. Little or no light will be visible from the glass, but a green glow will appear across the paper.

Fig. 28-1. *Shine a light into the edge of the glass and a light will glow at the other end.*

The light from the flashlight enters the edge of the glass and is reflected back and forth inside until it comes out the opposite edge and strikes the sheet of paper. When the light rays leave the flashlight, they are travelling nearly straight into the edge of the glass. The rays pass through the surface of the edge and are refracted inside. Once inside the glass, the rays strike the inside surface of the top and bottom at such an angle that they cannot pass through, but are reflected back into the glass. This continues until the rays come out, refracted at the other edge. Fiberoptics operate on this principle of internal reflection.

A fiberoptic cable is made up of a glass fiber covered with another layer of glass or other material that reflects the light back into the cable. A ray of light entering one end of the cable will bounce down the fiber and come out the other end. A fiberoptic cable is flexible and can even be twisted without losing any of the light that is transmitted.

Experiment 29

How a Mirror Works

Look into a mirror and notice the image you see. For all practical purposes, the image you see will be yourself, but it is not the real image of you. Light rays seem to come from the image in the mirror but actually they come from you and travel to your eye by reflection from the surface of the mirror. What you see is a reflection of your image (Fig. 29-1).

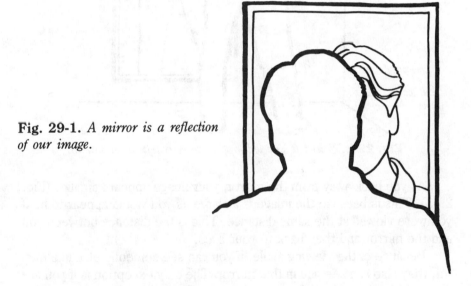

Fig. 29-1. *A mirror is a reflection of our image.*

We often think that a mirror reverses the image, but actually it doesn't. Standing in front of a full-length mirror, your left foot will appear on your left in the mirror and you will also appear right side up. We tend to think of the image in the mirror as an object instead of a reflection. If it was an object, it would be reversed, but being a reflection, your left hand will appear to your left and your right side will appear to your right (Fig. 29-2).

Fig. 29-2. *Your left side will appear to your left in the mirror.*

As you back away from the mirror, your image appears smaller (Fig. 29-3). This is because the image is as large as you would appear to be if you were viewed at the same distance. This is the distance between you and the mirror and then back to your eyes.

Because of the viewing angle, if you can see someone else in a mirror, they also can see you in that mirror. The only exception is if you are in the dark where there is no light to be reflected.

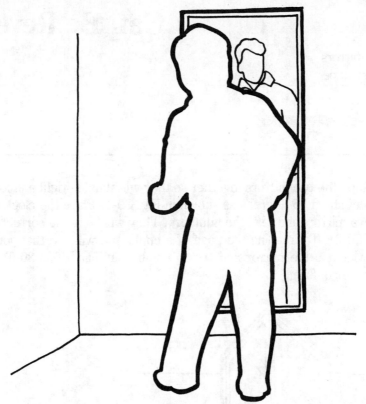

Fig. 29-3. *The reflected image becomes smaller as you back away.*

Experiment 30

How a Reflection Can Be Reversed

Materials

☐ 2 pocket mirrors
☐ transparent tape
☐ clock

Tape the two mirrors together so they will stand upright and form an angle of about 45 degrees as shown in Fig. 30-1. Place the clock facing the two mirrors and read the numbers. They will be in the correct order (Fig. 30-2). Try reading the page of a book. You will see that you can. Now, look in the mirror and try to comb your hair (Fig. 30-3). This might be confusing.

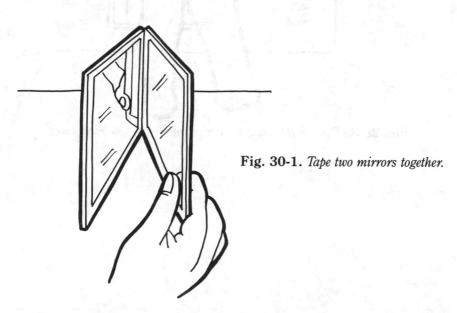

Fig. 30-1. *Tape two mirrors together.*

Light travelling from the left side of your face travels to the left mirror, which is reflected to the right mirror and then back again to your eye. Light travelling from the right side makes the same trip in reverse and is reflected back from the mirror on the left. This is the way you appear to others instead of the way you see yourself in the mirror. This is an image opposite to the one from a single mirror.

Fig. 30-2. *Stand a clock in front of the mirrors and read the numbers.*

Fig. 30-3. *Combing your hair in these mirrors might be difficult.*

Experiment 31

Materials

☐ large, shiny spoon

How a Mirror Can Produce Distorted Images

Look at your reflection from the back and the front of a shiny spoon. Compare the images. The back of the spoon curves outward and produces a smaller image while the front of the spoon curves inward and produces a larger image (see Figs. 31-1 and 31-2). The image is also inverted because the curve is deep. This is the same effect seen in Experiment 30 with the two mirrors.

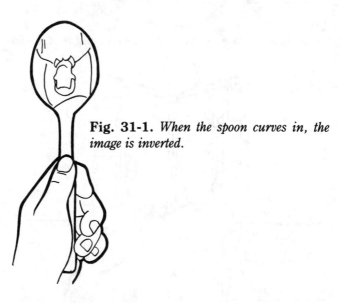

Fig. 31-1. *When the spoon curves in, the image is inverted.*

Mirrors that curve outward are called convex mirrors. They are often used as rear view mirrors on cars because light is reflected from a wide area behind the car. This produces a smaller image but gives the driver a wider field of view.

The mirrors that curve inward are called concave mirrors. They are found in homes and are used as shaving and makeup mirrors. The curve is very slight so the image is not inverted. Large concave mirrors are also used to make powerful reflecting telescopes.

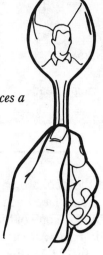

Fig. 31-2. *The back of the spoon produces a smaller, upright image.*

Mirrors that you find in fun houses at fairs and amusement parks are partly convex and partly concave. They produce both narrow and wide images on the same mirror.

Experiment 32

Using Mirrors to Multiply Reflections

Materials

☐ 2 pocket mirrors
☐ 2 hardback books
☐ marble
☐ spool from sewing thread

Place the books on a table about a foot apart. Align the books so that their fronts face each other. These will be the supports for the mirrors. Partly raise one of the covers and stand a mirror upright against the edge of the pages. Rest the cover on the top of the mirror to hold it in place (see Fig. 32-1). Repeat the steps with the other mirror so that you

Fig. 32-1. *Place the books facing each other and use the covers to support the mirrors.*

have two mirrors facing each other. Place the marble on the spool and set it an equal distance between the mirrors as shown in Fig. 32-2. Sight over one mirror into the other. You might have to adjust the angle a little. When both are aligned, you will be able to see a number of marbles, gradually getting smaller and disappearing into the mirror (see Fig. 32-3).

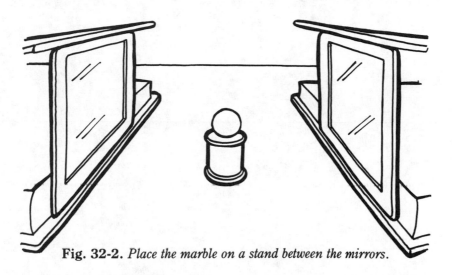

Fig. 32-2. *Place the marble on a stand between the mirrors.*

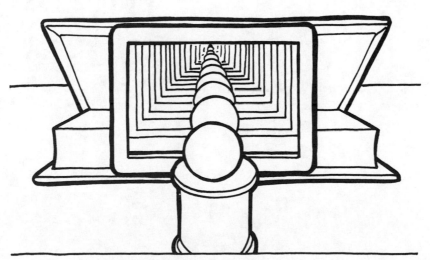

Fig. 32-3. *The mirrors multiply the reflections.*

The light from the marble causes its image to be reflected back and forth many times. The distance the reflection travels increases so the image becomes smaller. As the images are reflected, they also become dimmer. This is because a little of the light energy is consumed during each reflection.

Experiment 33

A Double Image from Glass

Materials

- ☐ piece of thick, plate glass
- ☐ sheet of black paper
- ☐ flashlight

Lay the black paper on a table and place the glass on top. Shine the flashlight so that the beam strikes the glass at an angle as shown in Fig. 33-1. Two circles of light will be reflected, one slightly misaligned with the other.

Fig. 33-1. *Place a piece of thick, plate glass on black paper, shine the light at an angle, and two circles will appear.*

Light rays travelling from the flashlight strike the surface of the glass and are reflected back up, but some of the light passes through the surface and is refracted to the bottom surface. There, it is reflected back up, passes through the surface, and travels alongside the other rays to your eyes.

Experiment 34

Reflecting Beams of Light

Materials

☐ comb
☐ mirror
☐ sheet of white paper
☐ bright sunlight

Place the paper on a flat surface in the sunlight. Hold the comb with the teeth down on the paper. Position it so that the sunlight makes beams of light from the comb fall across the paper (see Fig. 34-1). Place the mirror diagonally in the path of these beams (see Fig. 34-2). They will be reflected at an angle towards the edge of the paper. Notice the angle the beams strike the mirror and the angle they are reflected. Turn the mirror to different angles and notice the reflected beams.

Fig. 34-1. *Place the comb so that the light rays fall across the paper.*

Light is reflected from a mirror at exactly the same angle it strikes the mirror. When the angle of the mirror is changed, the reflected beams change to the same angle.

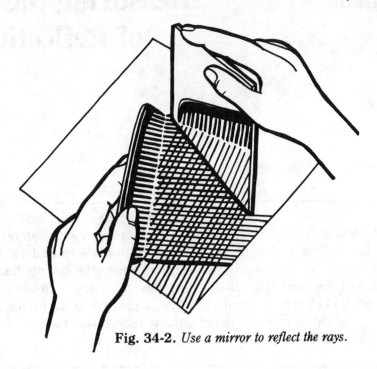

Fig. 34-2. *Use a mirror to reflect the rays.*

Experiment 35

Measuring the Angle of Reflection

Materials

☐ mirror
☐ sheet of paper
☐ protractor
☐ ruler
☐ pencil

Draw a dotted line down the center of the paper for a reference line (Fig. 35-1). Draw a straight line at any angle from the dotted line (Fig. 35-2). Place the mirror upright at the point where the straight line and the dotted line meet (Fig. 35-3). Move the mirror and align the dotted line with its reflection in the mirror. Next, sighting into the mirror, align the edge of the ruler on the paper with the reflection of the straight line and draw this line (Fig. 35-4).

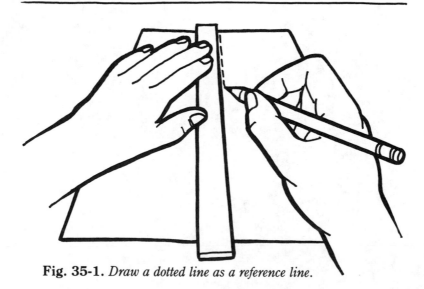

Fig. 35-1. *Draw a dotted line as a reference line.*

Compare the angles of each straight line with the dotted line (Fig. 35-5). Repeat the experiment using different angles. The protractor should show that light is reflected at the same angle it strikes the reflecting surface.

Fig. 35-2. *Draw a solid line across the reference line.*

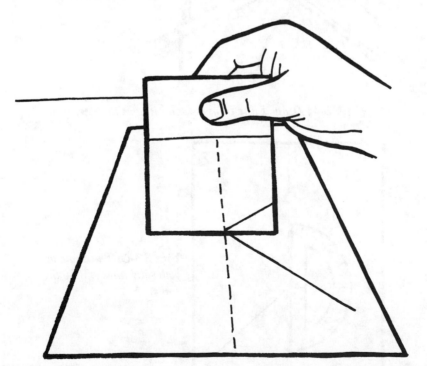

Fig. 35-3. *Place the mirror where the lines cross and line up the dotted line in the mirror.*

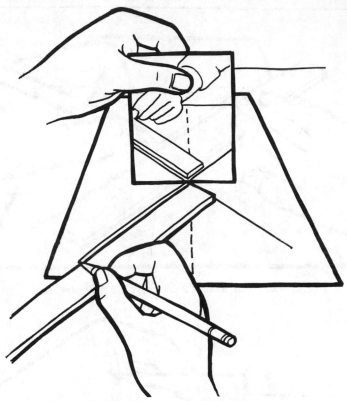

Fig. 35-4. *Draw a line from the solid line in the mirror.*

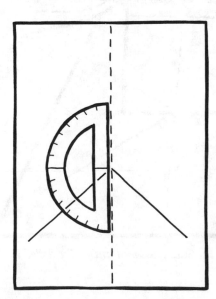

Fig. 35-5. *The angle of both solid lines will be the same.*

Experiment 36

How to Build
a Kaleidoscope

Materials

- ☐ 3 identical pocket mirrors
- ☐ transparent tape or masking tape
- ☐ small piece of wax paper
- ☐ tiny pieces of different colored paper
- ☐ lamp

Face the mirrors in and tape them together to form a triangle (see Fig. 36-1). Cut a triangle out of the wax paper and fasten it over one end with the tape (see Fig. 36-2). Drop the pieces of colored paper inside (Fig. 36-3). Stand near a lamp and look down through the kaleidoscope to see the pattern of colors (Fig. 36-4). Slight shaking will produce an endless variety of patterns.

The kaleidoscope works on the principle of multiple reflection. The light from the lamp shines through the tiny pieces of colored paper and are reflected in the mirrors. When the kaleidoscope is shaken, the pieces of colored paper move and the patterns change.

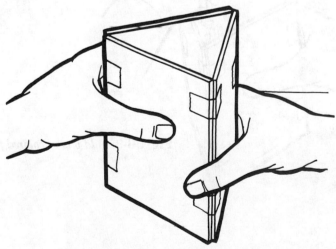

Fig. 36-1. *Tape three mirrors together.*

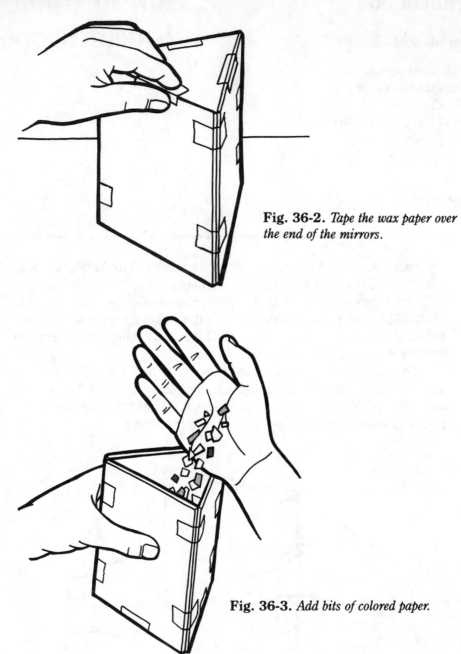

Fig. 36-2. *Tape the wax paper over the end of the mirrors.*

Fig. 36-3. *Add bits of colored paper.*

Fig. 36-4. *Look at the light, and you will see colored patterns.*

Experiment 37

Materials

- [ ] quart milk carton or similar size box
- [ ] 2 pocket mirrors
- [ ] transparent tape or masking tape
- [ ] utility knife

How to Make a Periscope

Carefully cut the top from the carton (or have an adult do it), then cut an opening in one side of the box near the top (see Figs. 37-1 and 37-2). Never cut with an object held against yourself, you could slip and seriously injure yourself. Cut another opening on the opposite side

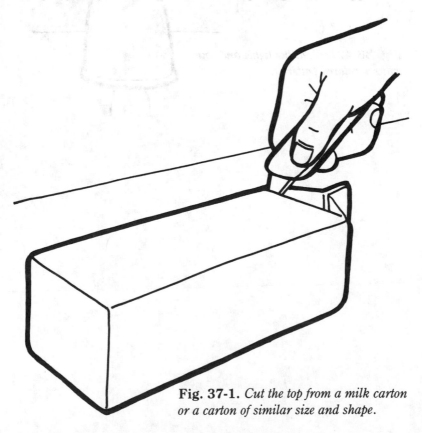

Fig. 37-1. *Cut the top from a milk carton or a carton of similar size and shape.*

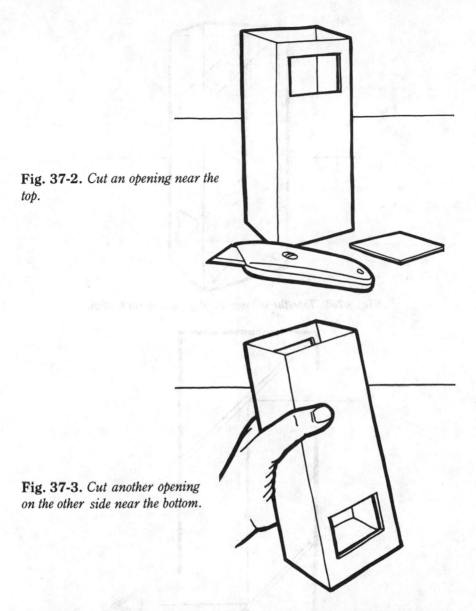

Fig. 37-2. *Cut an opening near the top.*

Fig. 37-3. *Cut another opening on the other side near the bottom.*

about the same distance from the bottom (Fig. 37-3). Place the mirror face up in the bottom at a 45 degree angle from the bottom opening as shown in Fig. 37-4. Tape the mirror in place. Next, mount the upper mirror face down at a 45 degree angle to the top opening. Tape this mirror in place.

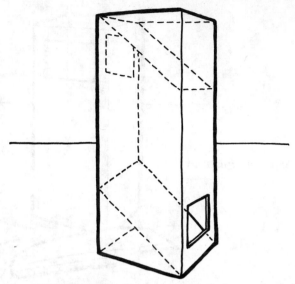

Fig. 37-4. *Tape the mirrors in place facing each other.*

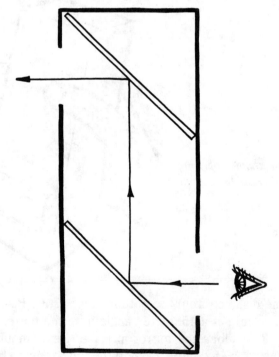

Fig. 37-5. *Mount each mirror at a 45 degree angle.*

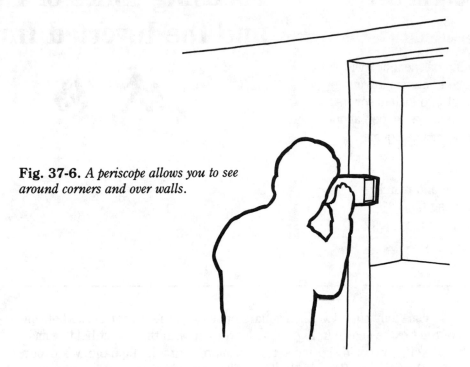

Fig. 37-6. *A periscope allows you to see around corners and over walls.*

Hold the periscope with the top opening just past the corner of a wall and look into the bottom opening (Figs. 37-5 and 37-6). You can see around the corner. Light travels from the object to the top mirror and is reflected down to the bottom mirror then reflected once again to your eye. Submarines are equipped with periscopes to let them see above the water.

Experiment 38

Focusing Lines of Light and the Inverted Image

Carefully cut a two-inch square opening in the center of the bottom of the box as shown in Fig. 38-1. Never cut with the object held against yourself, you could slip and seriously injure yourself. Tape the wax paper over this opening (Fig. 38-2). This will be the viewing screen. Cut a one-inch square opening in the center of the lid (Fig. 38-3). Tape the aluminum foil over this opening (Fig. 38-4). Using the needle, make a small opening in the center of the aluminum foil (Fig. 38-5). This is where the lines of light will cross.

Carefully light the candle and place it on a table in a dark room. Remember, hot wax can burn, so be cautious. Aim the end of the box with the pinhole at the candle (Fig. 38-6). Hold the box about 4 inches from the candle and slowly move it back and forth until a clear image appears on the wax paper. The image will be sharp but it will be upside down (Fig. 38-7) because light travels in a straight line through the pinhole.

This happens because the light travelling from the top of the candle travels through the pinhole and strikes the bottom of the wax paper, while light from the bottom of the candle travels through the pinhole to the top of the wax paper. Be sure to extinguish the candle and wait until it cools before attempting to move it. The pinhole acts as a lens and the image is inverted. The same thing happens in our eyes. The image is formed inverted on the back part of our eye. Our brain turns the image right side up.

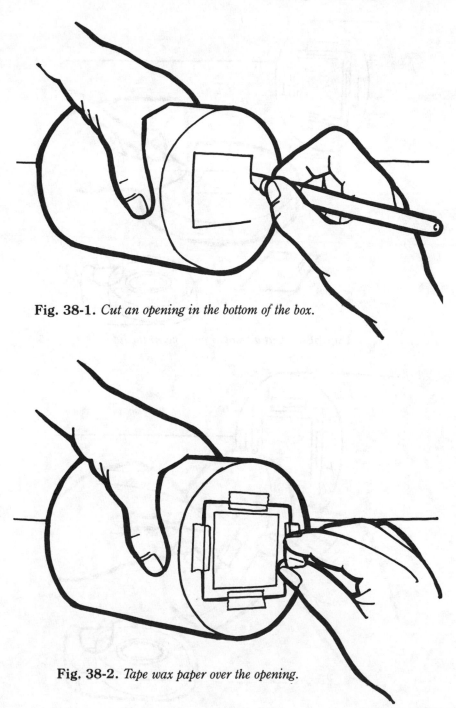

Fig. 38-1. *Cut an opening in the bottom of the box.*

Fig. 38-2. *Tape wax paper over the opening.*

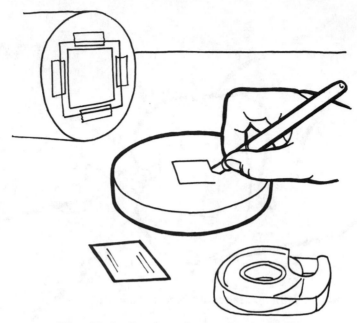

Fig. 38-3. *Cut a smaller opening in the lid.*

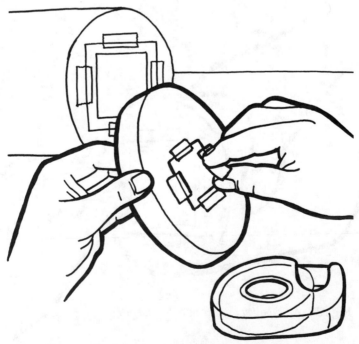

Fig. 38-4. *Tape aluminum foil over this opening.*

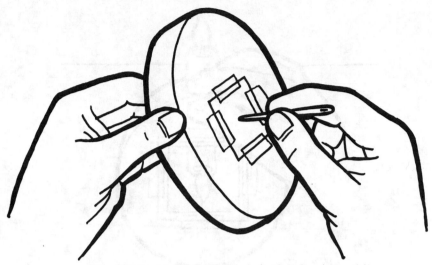

Fig. 38-5. *Make a small hole in the aluminum foil.*

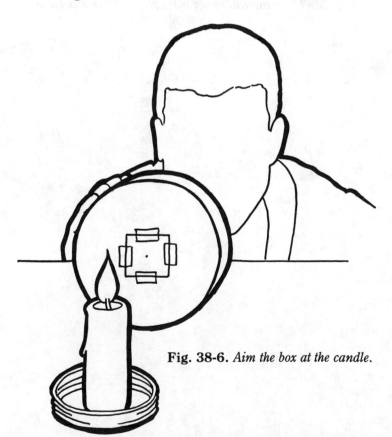

Fig. 38-6. *Aim the box at the candle.*

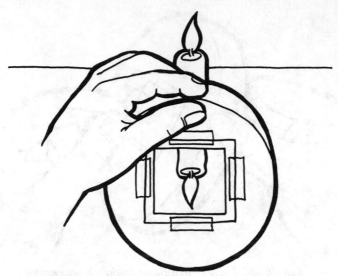

Fig. 38-7. *An inverted image will appear on the wax paper.*

Experiment 39

Materials

- ☐ round oatmeal box
- ☐ piece of aluminum foil (about two inches square)
- ☐ needle
- ☐ masking tape
- ☐ dull, black paint
- ☐ paint brush
- ☐ old newspapers
- ☐ roll of 120 black and white film (slow speed)
- ☐ scissors
- ☐ utility knife
- ☐ sunny day
- ☐ watch with second hand

Make sure all dust and cereal particles have been removed from the box. Carefully cut a one-inch square opening in the center of the side of the box (Fig. 39-1). Never cut with an object held against yourself.

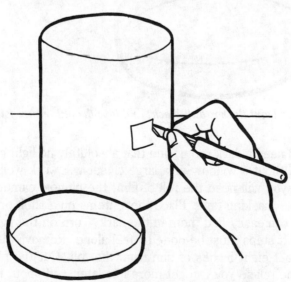

Fig. 39-1. *Cut an opening in the side of the box.*

Spread old newspapers on a table or countertop and paint the inside and outside of the box and the lid with dull black paint. Allow the paint to dry. Smooth the aluminum foil on a flat surface to remove any wrinkles and make a tiny hole in the center with the point of the needle. The hole should be only a little larger than the size of a hair. Position the aluminum foil on the outside of the box with the pinhole in the center of the one-inch opening. Carefully fasten it in place with the masking tape (Fig. 39-2). Securely tape all edges of the aluminum foil to prevent unwanted light from leaking in.

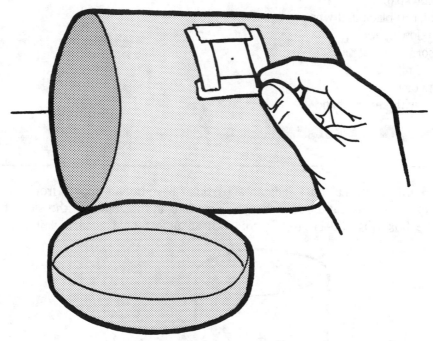

Fig. 39-2. *Paint the box dull black, and tape the aluminum foil in place.*

You will need a dark room, one that absolutely no light can get in. A bathroom without a window or a large closet will work well. Inside the dark room, you will need the roll of film, the pinhole camera, the scissors, and the masking tape. Place these items on a shelf or countertop so that you can easily find them in the dark. Turn off the light.

The next steps must be done by feel alone. Remove the roll of film and pull about eight inches of film from the roll. Cut the film about an inch from the roll so you can get more film later. Cut about three inches from the other end. This is the end that sticks out of the roll. This should leave you a curved strip of film about four inches long as shown in Fig. 39-3. Place this strip inside the box on the side opposite the pinhole (see Fig. 39-4). The curve of the film should fit the curve of the box. Tape the edges down with masking tape. Replace the lid and tape it in place to keep out unwanted light (Fig. 39-5). Replace the remainder of the film in its plastic, light-tight container for later. Hold your hand over the pinhole and take your camera outside into bright sunlight. Pick out a subject and place the camera on a solid surface to hold it steady.

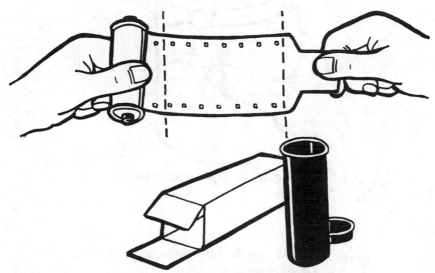

Fig. 39-3. *Cut a strip of film from the roll.*

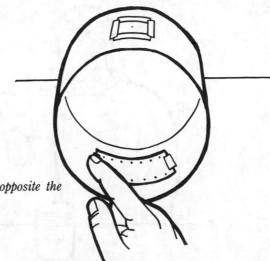

Fig. 39-4. *Tape the film opposite the pinhole.*

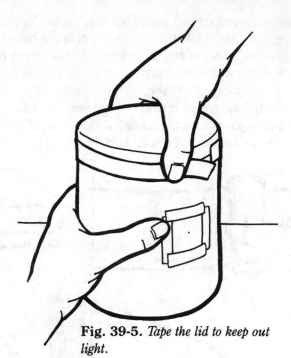

Fig. 39-5. *Tape the lid to keep out light.*

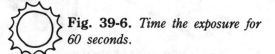

Fig. 39-6. *Time the exposure for 60 seconds.*

Remove your hand from the pinhole for an exposure of about 60 seconds (Fig. 39-6). Place your hand back over the pinhole and take the camera back into the dark room. Remove the film strip and place it in the plastic, light-tight container (Fig. 39-7). Press the snap-on lid in place. Have the film developed and a print made. Exposure time will vary with different light conditions.

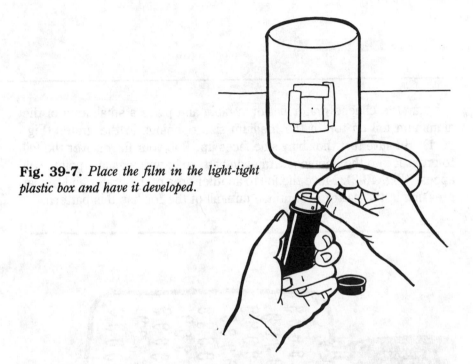

Fig. 39-7. *Place the film in the light-tight plastic box and have it developed.*

Light rays travel from the subject through the pinhole and strike the film attached to the other side of the box. The image is inverted because light travels in a straight line. This causes the light from the top of the subject to strike the bottom part of the film. Light from the bottom of the subject strikes the top part of the film. The film is sensitive to light and reacts to the image in front of the pinhole. When the film is developed a negative image is produced. The negative is then used to print the picture.

Experiment 40

How to Make a Reflector for Photography

Materials

- ☐ aluminum foil (12 × 24 inches)
- ☐ cardboard (10½ × 22½ inches)
- ☐ flat cheese grater
- ☐ glue

Lay the cheese grater flat on a table and place a small area of the aluminum foil on top of the medium size openings in the grater (Fig. 40-1). Be sure that the shiny side faces up. Rub your finger over the foil to press it into the openings. An even pattern of wrinkles and points will appear (Fig. 40-2). Move the foil to another area of the grater and repeat pressing in the pattern. Continue until all of the foil has this pattern.

Fig. 40-1. *Use a flat cheese grater to make the pattern.*

Apply a thin layer of glue to the cardboard and place the foil on the cardboard with the shiny side up. Wrap the edges around the back and glue them in place (Fig. 40-3). Allow to dry, and you have a reflector.

When you take a picture in bright sunlight, use the reflector to eliminate any harsh shadows on a person's face (Fig. 40-4). The reflected light will be soft and defused because of the wrinkled pattern.

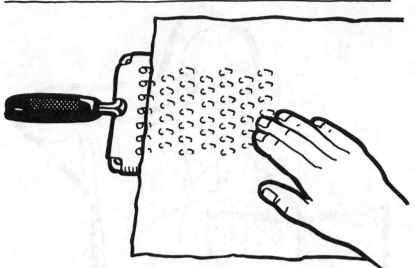

Fig. 40-2. *Press the aluminum foil to the cheese grater.*

Fig. 40-3. *Wrap the aluminum foil over the edges of the cardboard.*

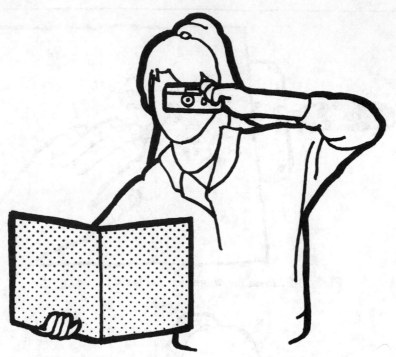

Fig. 40-4. *The reflector can be used to eliminate harsh shadows while taking photos in bright light.*

Experiment 41

The Water Magnifying Lens

Bend a round loop about ¹/₄ inch in diameter in one end of the wire. Use the pointed end of a pencil for a guide (see Fig. 41-1). Wrap the wire around the pencil and twist the wires together. Dip the wire loop in the bowl of water and slowly remove it (Fig. 41-2). Water will stay inside the loop. This is the lens.

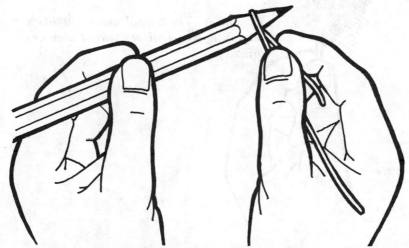

Fig. 41-1. *Make a round loop in the end of the wire. A pencil is a good support.*

Look through the lens at a printed page or examine the texture of a piece of fabric (Fig. 41-3). The circle of water acts like a magnifying lens. Most lenses are made of glass, but any transparent material can be used. In this case, both sides of the water lens curve outward and form a double convex lens. Double convex lenses are used in magnifying glasses.

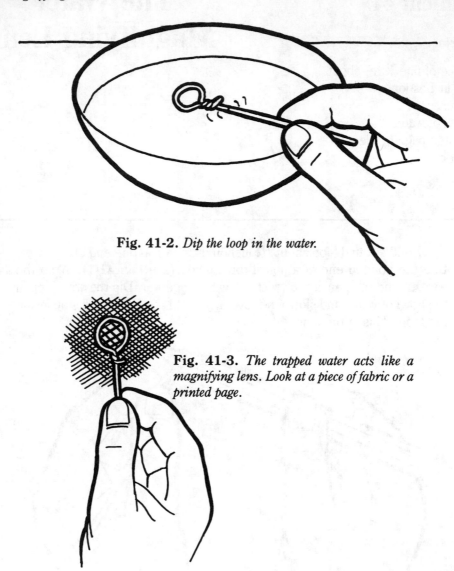

Fig. 41-2. *Dip the loop in the water.*

Fig. 41-3. *The trapped water acts like a magnifying lens. Look at a piece of fabric or a printed page.*

Experiment 42

How to Make an Ice Lens

Have an adult boil the water to get rid of the air in it and set it aside to cool a little (Fig. 42-1). It is important for the ice to be clear and free of air bubbles. Pour about a ¼ inch or so of water into the bottom of each glass (Fig. 42-2). Place both glasses in the freezer and freeze the water (Fig. 42-3). After the ice is frozen solid, take the glasses from the freezer and remove the curved pieces of ice (Fig. 42-4). Rub the top surface of the ice across a warm, flat surface to smooth out any rough spots. This will allow the two halves to fit together evenly (Fig. 42-5).

Fig. 42-1. *Have an adult boil the water to remove the air.*

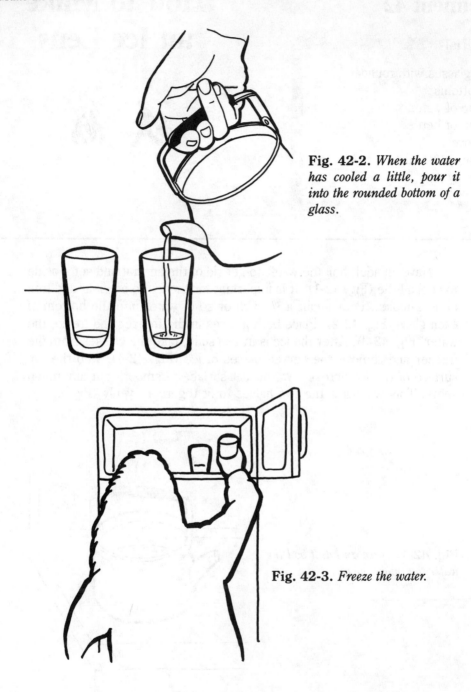

Fig. 42-2. *When the water has cooled a little, pour it into the rounded bottom of a glass.*

Fig. 42-3. *Freeze the water.*

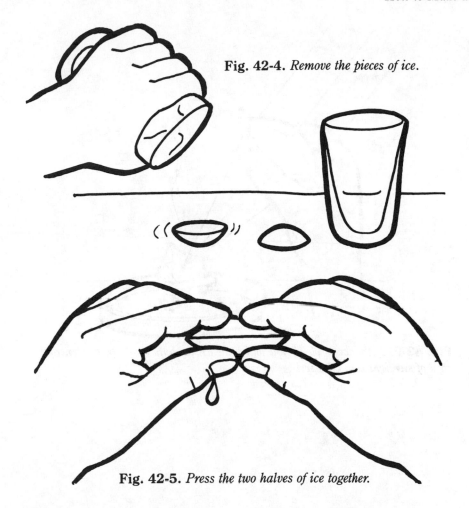

Fig. 42-4. *Remove the pieces of ice.*

Fig. 42-5. *Press the two halves of ice together.*

Press the two flat surfaces together into one lens that is curved on both sides—a convex lens. When pressing the two halves together, the increased pressure causes the ice to melt where the halves come together. When you release the pressure the ice quickly refreezes, sticking them together.

On a sunny day, take your lens outside and focus the rays of sunlight on a crumpled piece of paper (Fig. 42-6). Place the paper in a pan to avoid any fire hazards. If the lens is clear, you might be able to start a fire. If not, you should be able to at least brown the paper.

Light passing through a convex lens can be sharply focused. This concentration of light rays produces a great amount of heat.

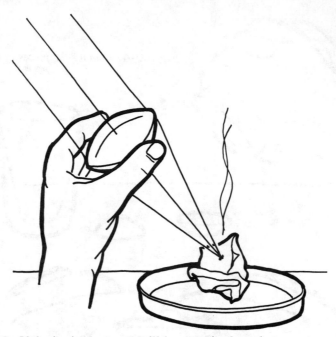

Fig. 42-6. *If the ice is clear, you will have an ice lens that can concentrate the rays of sunlight very effectively.*

Experiment 43

Finding the Focal Length of a Lens

Materials

☐ magnifying lens
☐ sheet of paper
☐ ruler
☐ compass
☐ pencil
☐ sunny day

Hold the magnifying lens in the sunlight and focus the rays to a fine point on a piece of paper. Place the point of the compass on the spot and spread the point of the pencil to touch the center of the lens as shown in Fig. 43-1. Measure this distance with the ruler (Fig. 43-2). This is approximately the focal length of the lens.

Because of the great distance to the sun, rays of light strike the lens in straight parallel lines. The curved lens bends the rays. The focal length of the lens is the distance between the lens and where the bent rays come to a point.

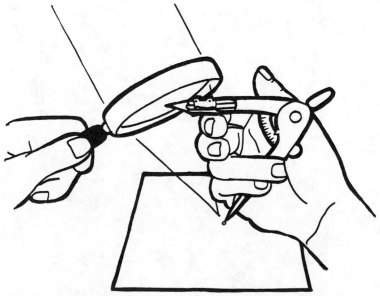

Fig. 43-1. *Use a compass to find the distance between the lens and the paper.*

Fig. 43-2. *Measure this distance to find the focal length of the lens.*

Experiment 44

Generating Heat from a Magnifying Mirror

Materials

☐ shaving or makeup mirror
☐ sunny day
☐ piece of crumpled paper in a metal pan
☐ jug of water

Face the mirror toward the sun and focus the reflected rays to a bright spot on the paper. The distance to the paper might be about two feet (see Fig. 44-1). Try to hold the mirror steady. You might need a box or something for a support. After a few minutes, and if the sun is bright enough, the paper will begin to smoke and might catch fire. If it does catch fire, extinguish it immediately with the jug of water.

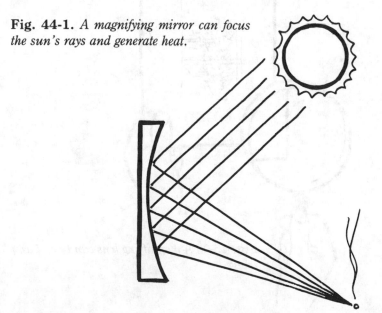

Fig. 44-1. *A magnifying mirror can focus the sun's rays and generate heat.*

When light passes through a convex lens, the light rays go through the glass and are bent to a point by refraction. If the mirror curves in, however, it is concave. In this case, the light rays don't pass through, but are bent to a focal point by reflection.

Experiment 45

Materials

- ☐ magnifying glass
- ☐ sunlight
- ☐ window
- ☐ sheet of white paper

Using a Magnifying Glass to Produce an Image

Hold the magnifying glass about 12 inches from the sheet of paper. The lens should be facing toward the window but not in the direct sunlight. Focus the lens until an image of the window and the landscape outside appears on the paper (Fig. 45-1). The image will also be upside down.

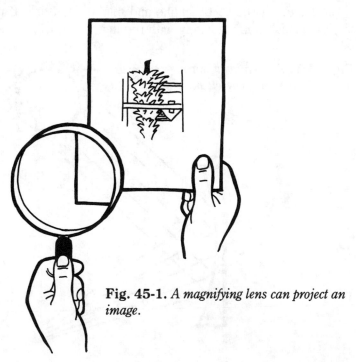

Fig. 45-1. *A magnifying lens can project an image.*

In this case, light rays travelling through the lens continue almost in a straight line like the camera lens. The light from the upper part of the window creates the light for the lower part of the image on the paper. The light from the bottom part produces the top part of the image.

118

Experiment 46

Materials

- ☐ magnifying glass
- ☐ sheet of white paper
- ☐ window
- ☐ large, hardback book
- ☐ transparent tape
- ☐ sunlight
- ☐ table

Lens Refraction of a Magnifying Glass

Tape the paper to the back of the book. Open the book so that it will stand upright on the table. Face the paper toward the window. Position the magnifying glass about 12 inches in front of the paper, out of direct sunlight.

Move the magnifying glass back and forth until a full image of the window appears on the paper. After you have a sharp image, slowly pass

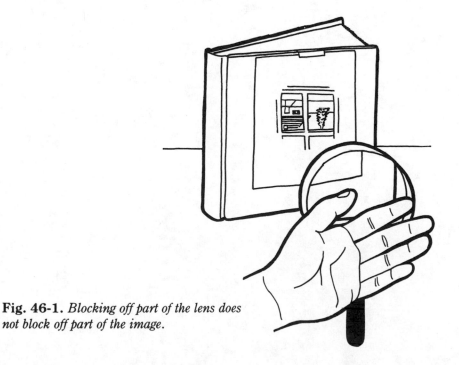

Fig. 46-1. *Blocking off part of the lens does not block off part of the image.*

one finger in front of the glass. Notice that the image only gets a little dimmer. Now, cover the top half of the lens with your hand. You would expect the bottom half of the image to disappear. Try covering the bottom half of the lens (Fig. 46-1). The full image of the window still remains on the paper. It is only dimmer. The light rays coming from the window and passing through the lens are refracted from so many angles that a full image will appear, but because half of the light was blocked off the image is not as bright or distinct.

Experiment 47

How a Reflecting Telescope Works

Materials

- [ ] curved, shaving or makeup mirror
- [ ] flat pocket mirror
- [ ] magnifying glass
- [ ] moonlight

Place the shaving mirror by a window so that the magnifying side faces toward the moon. Position the flat mirror facing the shaving mirror so that you can see a reflection of the moon in the flat mirror. Now look through the magnifying glass at the image of the moon in the flat mirror. It should appear much closer (Fig. 47-1).

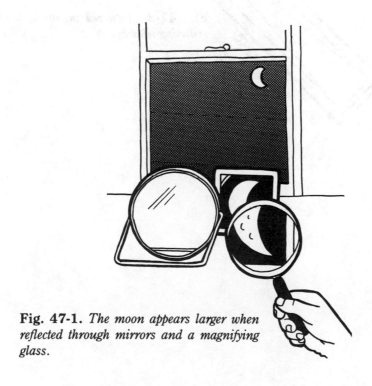

Fig. 47-1. *The moon appears larger when reflected through mirrors and a magnifying glass.*

Light travelling from the moon strikes the curved surface of the shaving mirror and is then reflected to the small flat mirror where it is again reflected through the magnifying lens (Fig. 47-2). The larger, curved mirror gathers light and concentrates it on the flat mirror. The lens magnifies the image. Isaac Newton, an English mathematician and physicist, constructed the first reflecting telescope.

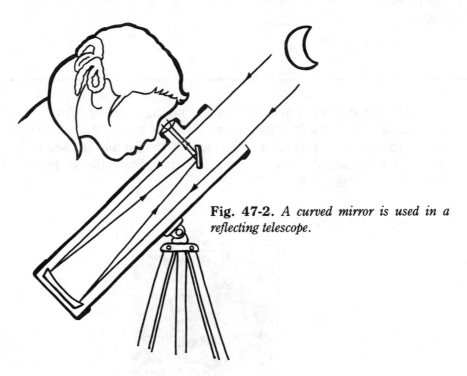

Fig. 47-2. *A curved mirror is used in a reflecting telescope.*

Experiment 48

How to Build a Refracting Telescope

Lenses can be obtained from old cameras, magnifying glasses, or other optical devices. The size of the cardboard tubes depend a lot on how large the lenses are. Mailing tubes or tubes from paper towels can be used. If these are not the right size, tubes can be rolled from cardboard or poster board.

Cut out two round cardboard disks to hold the small lens. Cut holes in the disks slightly smaller than the diameter of the lens. Glue one of the sides just inside one end of the smaller tube. Fit the lens in the end of the tube. Now place the other disk over the lens and fasten it in place with glue. Place the larger lens in one end of the larger tube. Position the tubes so that the lens will be at opposite ends of the two tubes. The smaller tube will need to slide smoothly in and out of the larger tube. Glue strips of felt around the outside of the smaller tube to fill in the gap. (See Fig. 48-1). Add enough layers so that it fits close but is still able to slide easily.

Light from the object being viewed is gathered by the larger lens called the objective lens. It is then focused on the smaller lens. The smaller lens, called the eyepiece, further magnifies the image.

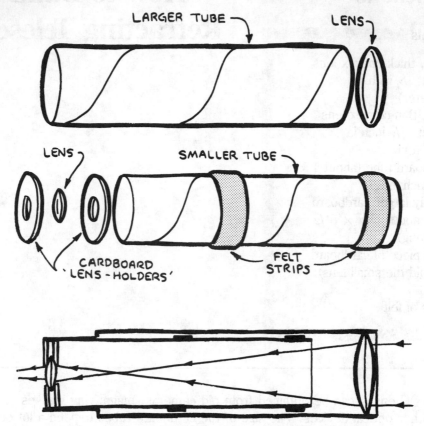

Fig. 48-1. *A refracting telescope made from cardboard tubes.*

Experiment 49

How to Build a Stroboscope

Materials

- ☐ sheet of cardboard or poster board ($8^1/_2 \times 11$ inch)
- ☐ empty, wooden spool from sewing thread
- ☐ round pencil or wooden dowel
- ☐ thumb tack
- ☐ small washer
- ☐ wood glue
- ☐ paint brush
- ☐ old newspapers
- ☐ dull, black paint
- ☐ saw
- ☐ compass
- ☐ scissors
- ☐ utility knife
- ☐ candle wax or soap
- ☐ electric fan or bicycle wheel

Set the compass for a four-inch radius and draw an eight-inch circle on the cardboard. Keep the compass at four inches and mark off six divisions around the edge of the circle. Draw three lines across the circle from one point to another. These will separate the circle into six, equal pie-shaped parts.

Reduce the spread of the compass $^1/_4$ inch from four inches to $3^3/_4$ inches. Place the point of the compass in the center of the circle and make a small mark across each of the lines, $^1/_4$ inch from the edge. Now set the compass at $1^3/_4$ inches and make another small mark across the lines. The two marks should be about two inches apart. Using the utility knife, carefully cut a slit between the marks, never cut against yourself. Make the opening $^1/_4$ inch wide and 2 inches long. Repeat the steps making six slits in the circle. Then cut out the circle with the scissors. Refer to Fig. 49-1.

125

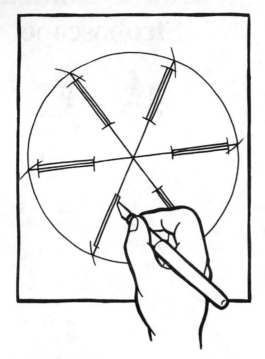

Fig. 49-1. *Cut slits in the disk.*

Carefully saw the spool in half and glue one end to the center of the disk (Figs. 49-2 and 49-3). Be sure to saw on a work table or vise. Have an adult help. The wide part of the spool should be glued, with the hole in the spool in the exact center of the disk. After the glue dries, spread old newspapers on a table or countertop and paint the disk and attached spool dull black. When the paint dries, coat the end of the pencil or wooden dowel with candle wax or soap and slide through the hole in the spool (Fig. 49-4). Put the point of the thumb tack through the washer and then through the center of the disk. Force the tack into the end of the pencil (Fig. 49-5). At this point, you should be able to hold the pencil in one hand and spin the disk with the other.

Hold the disk in front of your eyes and give it a spin. Look through the slits at the turning blades of an electric fan or a bicycle wheel. When the disk spins at the same speed as the fan blades, the blades will appear to stand still (Fig. 49-6). If the disk spins slower, the blades will appear to turn slowly. When the disk spins faster than the blades, they will seem to spin slowly, but in the wrong direction. The stroboscope allows us to study and observe things that happen at intervals too fast for the eye to see.

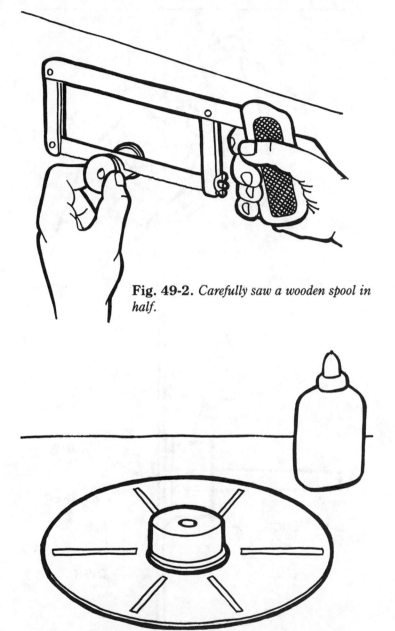

Fig. 49-2. *Carefully saw a wooden spool in half.*

Fig. 49-3. *Glue the spool to the disk and paint it dull black.*

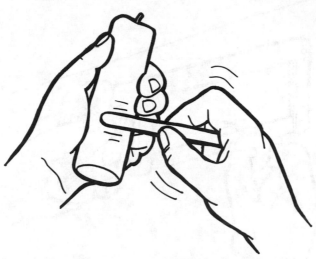

Fig. 49-4. *Rub wax or soap on the pencil to reduce friction.*

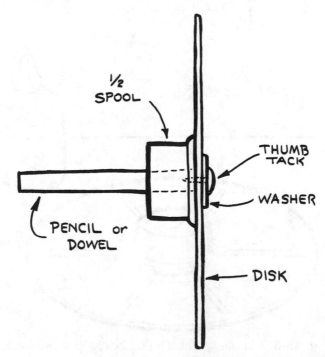

Fig. 49-5. *The disk is free to spin but is held in place with a tack and a washer.*

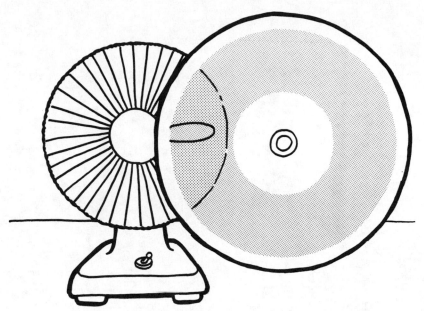

Fig. 49-6. *The spinning disk appears to stop a turning fan blade.*

SCIENCE FAIR PROJECTS

$\mathbf{A}$ science fair project can be an exciting adventure, but there are some important steps that should be followed. Probably the most important step that makes for a successful project is deciding on a suitable subject. Think of something that you are really interested in. Stay away from complicated projects that will be difficult for you to complete. It is hard to stay excited about a project that becomes tiresome and frustrating. It is important for the project to be enjoyable as well as educational. Take your time when choosing the subject and pick something you're very curious about.

After you have decided on a subject, break the project down into three steps—your hypothesis, your experiment, and your conclusions. Your project should answer a question or have a hypothesis. A hypothesis is simply what you think will happen as a result of the experiment. You will also want to tell people what you did during the experiment, perhaps in a report of the data you collected, or a display of your specimens. Finally, how you reached your results and your conclusions.

A report is normally included in a science fair project. It should include why you conducted the experiment. This should answer a question and then prove or disprove a hypothesis. It should show the way the experiment was performed, the results of the experiment and the conclusions. Often graphs and charts are useful in displaying this information.

The experiment should be about a specific problem or question. For example, how a magnifying glass magnifies an image should go into detail about how light rays are refracted or bent when they pass through a curved lens. You would want to demonstrate that light travels in a straight line until it passes through something different, glass, water, even layers of warm and cold air. You can show a curved lens bends the rays of light to a focal point.

If you are interested in how light flows in water, that experiment can be expanded into a luminous fountain (see Figure 1). Use a one-liter plastic bottle with the bottom cut out for a water reservoir. Mount it high to provide water pressure. Run a small flexible tube through a cork into the bottle to feed the fountain. You could make the fountain out of the glass tube from a medicine dropper inserted through a styrofoam container. Insert a drain tube to take the water to a bucket. Connect the flexible tube from the reservoir to the medicine dropper. Mount the fountain on a platform so a flashlight can stand underneath pointing up. The display should be in a darkened room. Turn on the flashlight and add water to the reservoir. You can add color by adding a few drops of food coloring to the reservoir.

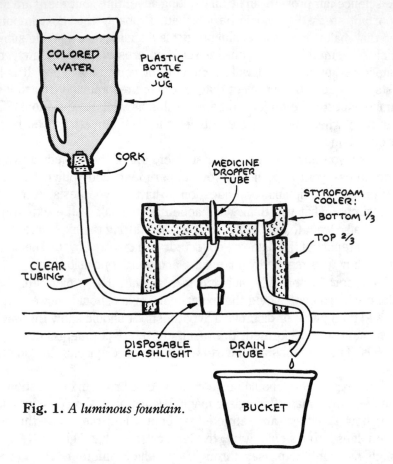

Fig. 1. *A luminous fountain.*

The experiment on the stroboscope can be improved by mounting the disk on a stand and turning it through a pulley and a hand crank (see Figure 2). A flashlight is attached to the stand to shine through the slits. Place the stroboscope in a dark room and hold the shutter open on a camera while someone makes rapid moves in the beam of light.

Different experiments will have to be made of different materials. Most projects can be made from wood and cardboard. You might start saving normal household throw-aways like wooden spools from thread, different shaped plastic and glass bottles, coffee cans, and cardboard tubes from paper towels.

You might want to display your project on a table in front of a self-supporting panel. The panel can be made of wood or cardboard. Each end should bend forward at a slight angle so it will stand by itself. This will also divide the panel into three sections. The section on the left can

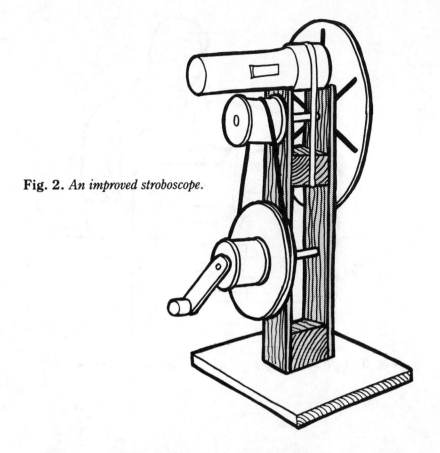

Fig. 2. *An improved stroboscope.*

show why the experiment was selected. The section in the middle can display diagrams and illustrations of the experiment and the section on the right might show the results and conclusions of the experiment (see Figure 3).

It is important to use your imagination and be creative, but the experiment doesn't have to be original. Just try to look at it from a different point of view. Ask yourself a lot of "what ifs." Most experiments have been done before, but you could use different materials, speeds, temperatures, or whatever. Fiberoptics started off rather simply but is now used in many areas from surgery to communications.

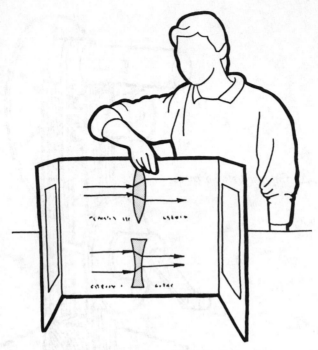

Fig. 3. *A self-supporting panel with illustrations of the experiment.*

Index